Further than the Furthest Thing

Zinnie Harris's plays include the multi-award-winning *Further than the Furthest Thing* (National Theatre/Tron Theatre; winner of the 1999 Peggy Ramsay Award, 2001 John Whiting Award, Edinburgh Fringe First Award), *How to Hold Your Breath* (Royal Court Theatre; joint winner of the Berwin Lee Award), *The Wheel* (National Theatre of Scotland; joint winner of the 2011 Amnesty International Freedom of Expression Award), *Nightingale and Chase* (Royal Court Theatre), *Midwinter*, *Solstice* (both RSC), *Fall* (Traverse Theatre/RSC), *By Many Wounds* (Hampstead Theatre) and *This Restless House* (National Theatre of Scotland/Citizens Theatre; Best New Play, Critics' Award for Theatre in Scotland, 2016). Her adaptations include Ibsen's *A Doll's House* for the Donmar Warehouse and Strindberg's *Miss Julie* for the National Theatre of Scotland. Zinnie received an Arts Foundation Fellowship for playwriting, and was Writer in Residence at the RSC, 2000–2001. She is Professor of Playwriting and Screenwriting at St Andrews University, and an Associate Director at the Traverse Theatre.

also by Zinnie Harris from Faber

ZINNIE HARRIS

Further than
the Furthest Thing

ff

FABER & FABER

First published in 2000
by Faber and Faber Ltd
74–77 Great Russell Street
London WC1B 3DA

Reprinted 2018

Typeset by Country Setting, Kingsdown, Kent CT14 8ES
Printed in England by CPI Group (UK) Ltd, Croydon CR0 4YY

A CIP record for this book
is available from the British Library

978-0-571-20544-8

Author's Note

Further than the Furthest Thing is set on a remote island
in the middle of the Atlantic, based loosely on the real
island of Tristan da Cunha. The island is as far from
Cape Town in one direction as South America in the
other, and its only contact with the outside world is a
ship that visits approximately every six months.
Although the year is 1961, the extreme isolation has
meant that the islanders are an odd hybrid of cultures
and periods, part Napoleonic, part Victorian and part
modern in dress, accent and attitude. The men wear
trousers, jackets and flat caps, the women patterned
dresses and head scarves. Both sexes wear very thick
white socks knitted from roughly spun sheep's wool.
The island community is around 170 people, made
from seven families descended from the original seven
shipwrecked sailors who started the colony centuries
before. There are neither electricity nor trees on the
island, so the houses are entirely lit by lamplight and
made of stone and planks salvaged from shipwrecks.

Further than the Furthest Thing owes much to the Tristan
islanders and their story, the story of their beautiful island
and isolated lifestyle that was dramatically interrupted
when the volcano erupted and the entire community was
evacuated to Southampton. However the story is not
solely their own and departs from accurate documentation
almost immediately. In many ways I stole the real Tristan
da Cunha to feed my imagination, and emerged gorged,
to write into existence a host of characters and events
that never happened. Anyone who is sufficiently interested
in discovering the true story of their evacuation and

history should take the time to read some of the many books that have been written about it – they will find the real version is richer still.

My own connection with Tristan da Cunha started when my grandfather, Dennis Wilkinson, was posted there as an Anglican priest soon after the Second World War. He took with him my grandmother, then a young woman, and my mother and aunt as children. Although they only spent a few years there, it went into family mythology, and we all grew up on tales of this magical place. We spent many evenings poring over hazy photographs of men with strangely serious faces, we were told about long boats, penguin eggs, black volcanic sand and places that were called things like 'The Patches' or 'The Ugly Road'. My mother still on occasion eats potato raw, claiming she prefers it, and she and my aunt can still remember being told about the 'H'outside Warld' as someone might tell a fairytale. It is to this Tristan, the Tristan of childhood memories, with fuzzy edges and missing bits, that this play is dedicated. And also, of course, to my Mum.

Zinnie Harris, June 2000

The Rain on Tristan da Cunha

The wet world drips
    and drips and drips.

This wealth of water wears
    down man's resolution;
    disables winged devotion;
    yet speaks of endless tears
    shed for a world of sin.

Christ weeps for Tristan,
    last stronghold of simplicity
    where now a pagan culture comes on fast,
    destroying faith and charity.
Ambitions' ultimate bounds are passed:
    Here comes the lust for gold at last!
    And hope is left us, thin
    and ailing, sick and pale;
    while worldly ill
    creeps in
    unasked, unwanted.

Christ for Tristan weeps:
    See how the wet world drips,
    and drips and drips . . .

Rev. Dennis Wilkinson, 1949

This Lonely Rock

Austere, this lonely Rock at the earth's end
Defies still all the astonished ocean;
Wildest winds of the southern heavens bend
Under this strong hand. Our Isle of Tristan
Fears not rebuke, but stands erect to face
These envious seas, unfriended. Surely none
Stronger in heart, this unexpected place,
Lost in uncharted waters, stands alone,
Immovable. Such might o'ertops the waves
And – as our Saviour Christ – stands fast,
Holds them in check, buffets them back, and saves
Us now – as He shall save us at the last.

To image thus our Lord, while time endure
Tristan da Cunha, may thy strength be sure.

Rev. Dennis Wilkinson, 1949

Further than the Furthest Thing, a co-production between the Tron Theatre Company, Glasgow and the Royal National Theatre, was was first performed at the Traverse Theatre, Edinburgh, on 6 August 2000. The cast, in order of speaking, was as follows:

Mill Lavarello Paola Dionisotti
Francis Swain Gary McInnes
Bill Lavarello Kevin McMonagle
Mr Hansen Darrell D'Silva
Rebecca Rodgers Arlene Cockburn

Cimbalom played by Greg Knowles

Director Irina Brown
Designer Niki Turner
Lighting Designer Neil Austin
Music Gary Yershon
Sound Designer Duncan Chave
Movement Director Jackie Matthews
Company Voice Work Patsy Rodenburg

Characters

Mill Lavarello
Francis Swain
Bill Lavarello
Mr Hansen
Rebecca Rodgers

FURTHER THAN THE FURTHEST THING

Act One

SCENE ONE

Bill is standing by the edge of the mountain lake.
He takes off his clothes and steps into the water. It is
very cold.
He reaches down to wet his arms and face.
He puts his shoulders under the surface and swims.
A terrible rumbling begins under the water.
The noise becomes more and more deafening.
Bill panics, trying to swim back to the shore. He nearly
drowns but manages to haul himself onto the bank.
After he has caught his breath he stands up and turns
around to look at the water . . .
There is silence.

SCENE TWO

Mill and Francis, inside Mill's house. They are in the
main room which is very bare apart from the walls
which are plastered with dated (1950s) magazine
cuttings.
Francis has just walked in.

Mill

Been waiting. Since sun is first come up.
I's seeing your ship from the first it was.
I's holding my breath for the rocks. Shutting my eyes
for the corner.
Counting my heart's beating as in it came.

Francis

Mill . . .

3

Mill

Don't come near, just as yet.
Let me be seeing you first
The other way
So these is what they is wearing, H'outside there
then?
Your uncle's been a missing you.
He's an old man. You shouldn't be as going off from
an old man.

Francis

Only been gone . . .

Mill

Months
Months and months
I is counted Francis
Is half the year and half again

Francis

There was no boat

Mill

Don't come near me, I's still looking at you.
Had two weddings
Two weddings
And lots of birthdays
Harry Repetto is died.
Missed that. See – missed Harry Repetto is died.
Is dead second Sunday after you left.
No one is ever leaving before
Not for a long time
You is always the first, is having to be, that's your
trouble.
Where's your bag?

Francis

On the shore

Mill

Might as being divided up with all the other things
that is come off the ship
Said don't touch me. I's still making sure it is you.

Pause.

A Hagan is married a Glass and a Hagan is married
a Green
And you is missed both.
And Harry Repetto . . .

Francis

Is that all is married?

Mill

Is two weddings Francis

Francis

She wasn't on the shore

Mill

She'll be along

*Mill looks around, awkward and wanting to find
something to show him.*
She indicates the walls.

Boat you left on is bringing us whole load of pictures.
Is all new Francis

Francis looks around at the walls.

Francis

I like it

Mill

Do you?
Is the Queen.
There.
As is sitting on her throne in H'England.
And that's some mountains somewhere
Is never seeing those mountains is you?

Francis

No

Mill

Is needing to look at them before saying 'No', Francis.

Francis

I didn't see those mountains

Mill

Anyway, is a mountain here.
No need to go away and see a mountain, we've got one here.
Just some pictures, Francis. I is taking them down soon.

Pause.

You wanting an H'egg?
Got one, is for you.
Could boil it up for you.

Francis

No thanks

Mill

Wouldn't be taking a second

Francis

I'm not hungry

Mill

Will be in a minute, mind.
You always is hungry. That's how I was telling myself as what you is like.
I was saying Francis, is always hungry.
I'll be heating up the water just now for you.

Francis

No Mill

Pause.

Mill

A cup of tea?

Francis

I'm fine as I am

Mill

The Queen is taking tea in the afternoon. And Prince Whats His Name.

Pause.

Where was you saying your bag was?

Francis

On the shore

Pause.

Mill

Can't be thinking what else there is. Must as be something else is happened. Your uncle be pleased to see you anyway.

I suppose you is seen the church?

Roof is pulled down to be making Harry Repetto's coffin. So that is that.

Church isn't being the same when the rain is running down your neck.

You is sure you is not wanting an H'egg?

Oh I know, you is not hungry.

Thinking of this bag of yours then –

We is needing to go and get it now, before the tide is coming up . . .

Francis

Mill?

Mill

What?

Francis

Am I allowed to come and kiss you yet?

7

Mill isn't sure as she goes towards him.
Then she almost bursts into tears as she hugs him.
Bill enters, looking confused.

Bill

Something in the water.

Mill mops her tears.

Bill

Something terrible under the water, underneath where it is dark. Mill I's heard something . . .

Mill

Bill?

She nods towards Francis.
Bill stops and sees Francis for the first time.

Francis

Hallo Uncle Bill.

Pause.

Bill

Francis.

Bill holds out both hands. Francis takes them, but they are awkward with each other.

Bill

Is something in the water lad

Mill

I was telling him that we's been missing him.

Bill

Heard it when I put my head under, like a great juddering . . .

Mill

He is just stepped off the boat

Bill

No time to waste Mill, might have gone by the time we's getting back there.

Mill

We's just going to get his bag

Bill stops.

Bill

His bag?

Mill

From the shore.

Bill

Can wait, can't it lad?

Francis

Maybe it was the wind

Bill

Was bigger than the wind, and under. Was under like a wave of thunder.

Mill

You never mind him Francis, is more like a fool every day

Bill

And when I came out, it was as like these hands were a pulling at me

Mill

Bill, in heaven's name. The lad is just walked off the boat after is gone for months and months

Bill

Francis look at me. My legs is shaking

Mill

You is carrying on like this and I is making you shake.

Francis

It's alright Aunty Milly

Bill

I was not even having time to let my clothes dry. I was
that scared, that I's just running down the hill.
Look at that.

Bill sits down and takes his shoes off.

Mill

He's as pleased to see you as I am. Underneath.

Bill

I's telling you there is something in the water.
Is something in the water

*Bill goes over to the table where there is a jug of water.
He holds it up to the light.*

Mill

He is been so excited about you coming

*Bill tastes the water. Then he puts his ear right up close
to the jug and listens.*
Mill wrings her hands.

Mill

Is having one of his off days.

Francis shrugs.

Francis

It doesn't matter.

Pause. They watch Bill, who is absorbed.

Francis

I've got a surprise for you

Mill

For me?

Francis

For all of you.

Mill

With my bag.
Down on the shore

Mill

Oh?

Francis

I'll go and get it.

Francis starts to leave, as he goes he steps back in.

Francis

Oh and Aunty . . .

Mill

Yes?

Francis

I's glad to be back.

*Bill is still muttering to the water and pouring it over his
fingers.*
Mill waits until Francis has gone, then turns on Bill.

Mill

You

Bill

What?

Mill

Going on like that

Bill

I's telling you there is . . .

Mill

I is not wanting to hear it Bill. Is months and months
away and is only just walked in the door, and you
is going on about . . .

Bill

I'm scared Mill.

Mill

Is rubbish

Bill

Is no good. Whatever it is. Is no good.

Pause.

Mill

You is always the same.

Francis and you. Ever since Francis is a boy you and he won't be looking at each other and saying, 'Is good to see you'. 'Is good to see you' . . . And do not be thinking that you is going anywhere, you is going nowhere until we is finished all sitting down and eating. Like a family.

Bill

But Mill . . .

Mill

You is staying right here

Bill stops what he is doing.

You can be going in the morning
Is been away for months and months . . .
Is good to see him, isn't it Bill?

Bill

Of course is good to see him

Pause.

Mill

Just because is not your family

Bill

No

Mill

When you is looking at him you's seeing Swain

Bill

I's seeing Francis

Mill

I's seeing my sister

Pause.

Bill

Of course is good to see him Mill

Mill

He's been away

Bill

I know

Mill

I's wanting it to be special

Mill takes the jug back and puts it on the table. Bill stands up.

Mill

I've got H'eggs

Bill says nothing.
Mill shows him three in a basket.

Mill

Pinnawin H'eggs

Bill

Milly?

Milly shrugs.

Mill

Tonight is as going to be special

Bill

Pinnawin?

Mill

They's had plenty

Bill

Who?

Mill

I is found them

Bill

You's shouldn't have gone touching them

Mill

They's wasn't in a nest

Bill

You's should have left them be

Mill

They's just on the path, left

Bill

They's have come back for them

Mill

Tonight is the night Francis is come home

Bill

It's bad luck to take a pinnawin one

Mill

Tch

Bill

We isn't needing any more bad luck
You should have been leaving them

Mill

Tastes nice though
Pinnawin H'eggs
Haven't had a Pinnawin H'egg since
Long long time
Since the day your pa is dead

Bill

We was having one then?

Mill

We all was.

Pause.

Shall I be taking them back now?

Bill
I don't know

Mill
Could easy

Bill gets out three plates.

Bill
Well now they're here.

Mill
You is a good man Bill Lavarello.

Pause.
They both start laying the table.

Mill
Francis was saying that he is got a surprise for us.

Bill
Oh

Mill
Surprise is as come from the H'outside World

Bill
Oh

Mill
Never been having a surprise before
Could be some more pictures.
Or some sugar
You remember when the last boat came and was
bringing us all some sugar?
Maybe is sugar?

Bill
Maybe is

Bill carries out the eggs and puts them in a pan.

Mill
You need to be putting water in the kettle Bill

Bill reluctantly goes to fill the pan with water.

Mill
Wait
They's beautiful

Bill
Was we really eating them the day my pa is died?

Mill
Yes

Bill
Fancy you is remembering that

Mill
Let me be holding one for a second

Bill offers her the pan. She takes one out.

Mill
Is still warm

She takes the other one out, so she is holding two, one in each hand.
She tries to take the third one out, but as she does so it rolls off her hand.
It smashes on the floor.
They stare at it.
Pause.

Bill
Now that is bad luck

Mill
Don't Bill

Bill
I'll get a cloth

Mill

Maybe we's could . . .

She attempts to scoop it up with the shells, still holding the other two eggs.

Bill

No

Mill

Is waste

Bill

Doesn't matter

Mill

Waste of a life, I mean
A little pinnawin is gone smash on our floor.

Bill

Mill?

Mill

I shouldn't have took it

Bill

I'll clear it up

Mill

Shouldn't have gone taking them should I?
I was so wanting it to be special

Bill

I know

Bill lifts the remaining two out of her hands and puts them in the pot.

Is two left Mill.
You and Francis have them

Mill

No no.
Not me

Bill

We can share them, they's big ones.
Plenty for us all Mill

Mill

I shouldn't have gone taken them anyway

Bill bends down and clears up the mess.

Mill

I is not seeing how they is bad luck.
They is only an H'egg. How can an H'egg be as bad
luck.
How can something is new life be as bad luck?

Bill

I don't know
Maybe is because it is new life and we's eating it as is
bad luck.

Mill

No one says that about crawfish. Or potatoes. They is
life isn't they?

Bill

Suppose

Mill

Anyway we's already had all our bad luck as is due us.

Bill stiffens as he puts the broken egg in the bin.
Mill goes back over to the pot.
She takes one out again.

Mill

Was just holding it to say is still warm.
Still warm Bill.

She takes the other one out.

Bill

Careful Mill

Mill

 I is careful

 You is wanting a hold?

Bill

 No

Mill

 Hold it Bill. Feel as is still warm.

Bill puts down the dustpan and brush and holds one.

Mill

 And th'other.

Mill hands over the other, but Bill doesn't have it
properly. He drops it.
They stare at the second broken egg.
Mill starts to wail.

Bill

 Doesn't matter

 Doesn't matter Mill. Is still one left, isn't there?

 That one we is kept for Francis.

 Francis is needing them, you and me isn't.

Bill is still holding the third egg

Mill

 I shouldn't have gone taking them

Bill

 Doesn't matter

Bill puts the third egg back in the pan.

Mill

 You is right, the adult birds would have come back

 for them, 'course they would.

 Imagine if that is me. If I's that bird and I's coming

 back and seeing them gone . . .

Bill says nothing, he just watches her.

Mill

Only it could never be me, could it?

Bill

Francis will be back soon.
He can have the last H'egg.

Bill puts the pan onto the stove.

Mill

He was saying he's got us a surprise

He sits her down.
He gets out three mugs and puts them on the table as he talks.

Bill

I was seeing you waiting today
I was seeing you from the mountain
I was seeing you standing on the shore
A tiny speck
But I was knowing it was you

Mill begins to lose her daze.

I was telling from the way you was standing that you was holding your breath.

Mill

I couldn't watch

Bill

I could tell.
You was shutting your eyes

Mill

I was not wanting to see

Bill

I could tell

Mill

Why didn't you come down?

Bill

I don't know

Mill

You could have been waiting with me

Bill

I was wanting to but . . .
I needed to swim.
The water was . . . I was wanting to.
I was needing to swim.

Mill

Oh.

Bill

Only then I was not able

Mill hears the sound of footsteps on the path.
She goes to the window.

Mill

Is coming back. Bill – is coming back. Is that boiling?

Bill

Boiling

Mill

Maybe it'll be sugar as brought us.
Big sack of sugar.

Francis comes back in. He is carrying a brown leather
briefcase, once smart, now worn.
Mill is surprised by how small it is.

Mill

That your bag?

Francis

I don't need much

Mill

Oh

Mill has a good look at the bag.

Mill
Isn't yours is it?

Francis
I was given it.

Bill
We's doing your H'egg

Francis
Thanks

Bill
Come and be sitting

Francis
It's strange to be back
Good and strange
It's like nothing has happened

Mill
Two weddings is happened
And Harry Repetto

Francis
Nothing is really happened.

Bill puts one egg-cup on the table.

Francis
Aren't you having one?

Bill
We has smashed them, as a mistake

Francis
Oh

Bill
One left, is for you

Francis
Thanks
I brought the surprise

Mill
Oh?

Francis
Well, it's a sort of surprise

Mill
Oh

Francis
Not a gift, just a . . .

Bill and Mill look surprised.

Francis
Someone I want you to meet. A friend of mine.
I brought him home with me

Francis goes to the door.

Francis
Come on.
Aunty Mill and Uncle Bill, this is Mr Hansen

Mr Hansen walks in.
Nobody says anything.

Francis
Take a seat

Mr Hansen brushes the chair then sits down.

Francis
Mr Hansen is from Cape Town

Pause. Mill and Bill don't like the look of him.

Mill
We only has one H'egg

Francis
Mr Hansen can have it

Mill
You must be having the H'egg Francis

Francis

Mr Hansen owns a factory in Cape Town.

Pause.

Francis

The largest factory in the whole of Cape Town

Pause.

Francis

When you arrive at the harbour it is the only thing
you can see, like a great giant staring up at you.
Then as you get closer you can see people and
machinery and windows and smoke, lots of smoke
And he employs thousands of workers. Don't you?
Thousands of people. And wherever you go in Cape
Town, everyone has heard of Mr Hansen.
And ask him what the factory makes. Go on ask him
what it makes.

Bill

What does it make?

Mr Hansen

Jars

Francis

Not just jars

Mr Hansen

And cans.

Francis

And boxes. All kind of boxes.

Mr Hansen

Containers generally

Bill

You must be needing a lot of containers in Cape Town.

Mr Hansen

We are.

Francis

Not just Cape Town, Mr Hansen has factories all
over the world.

Mr Hansen

Small factories

Mill

You is never making anything to be putting in the jars?

Mr Hansen

No

Mill

Oh

Sounds like is exciting

Never been hearing of a factory that made just jars.

Bill

I's afraid you's going to find us rather dull Mr Hansen.
There is no factories on the island. Just the
mountain and the patches.

Mr Hansen

Francis told me a little of what it would be like.

Bill

How long is you staying?

Mr Hansen

Two days.

Francis

Until the ship leaves again

Bill

Well you is welcome, isn't he Milly?

Francis

Mr Hansen is staying on the ship Uncle Bill.

Bill

Oh.

Mill

Are you going to eat that H'egg?

Pause.

Mill

Are you going to eat that H'egg?

Mr Hansen

Thank you, yes.

Mill

We did have more but they as got smashed. If we had
been knowing we was having guests this night, that
is to say not just Francis, we would have got more,
is as so Bill?
We is eating a lot of these kind of H'eggs up here.

Pause.

Mill

You is wanting a cup of tea to go with that Mr Hansen?

Mr Hansen

Thank you no.

Mill

I know you's maybe is thinking we is simple living as
like this, but we's from the island and we is used
to it. We is not needing any fancy stuff. We's got
potatoes hasn't we? And carrots and crawfish, and
four cows up by the school and even if as our
church hasn't got a roof just at the minute when
you is singing the way we is singing on the island,
who is needing a roof?

Pause.
Mr Hansen nods in agreement.

Mr Hansen

Indeed.

Mill

So don't you go wiping our chairs before you is sitting
down.

Pause.
Mr Hansen stands up.

Mr Hansen

I should be going.
Mr Swain. Mrs Swain

Mill

Lavarello
Francis is Swain. We is Lavarello

Mr Hansen

Apologies. Mrs Lavarello.
I should be getting back

Mill

You isn't finished your H'egg as yet

Mr Hansen isn't sure.

Mill

We doesn't go wasting things here either

Mr Hansen sits down.

Mr Hansen

It's a very beautiful island Mr Lavarello

Bill

We's knowing it.
None other is so beautiful I shouldn't think, whole of
the ocean.

Mill

Well finish it then

Bill

Leave him be Mill

Mill

I's only saying he's to finish it before it gets cold

Mr Hansen

Let me show you something

He eats the egg quickly by putting several mouthfuls in his mouth.
Mr Hansen holds up his empty eggshell to show them.
He swallows.

Mr Hansen

See, nothing there.

He places the egg on the table and smashes it into fragments with his fist.
He then takes out a handkerchief and puts the egg fragments into it.
He blows on the bundle.
Then he opens up the handkerchief again and produces a glass jar.
Mill gasps, Bill is more suspicious.

Mill

Where is the H'egg shell has gone?

Mr Hansen

Vanished

He shows her the handkerchief which is empty.
He also shows her his two hands and shows that there is nothing up his shirt sleeves.
Mill takes the jar and looks it over.

Mill

Is real
Look Bill, is real

Mr Hansen stands up again.

Mr Hansen

I really should be going now. You've been most kind.

Francis
There is no need

Mr Hansen
They lock up the ship at night

Mill
Let me see that cloth.

Mr Hansen hands her the cloth. Mill inspects it both sides.

Mill
Do it again

Bill
Mill be leaving him be, is having to get back now

Mill
You is not minding my asking are you Mr Hansen?

Mr Hansen
It's nothing really

Mill
They'll not be locking the ship without you.

Mr Hansen looks at Francis.

Mill
Francis will be walking you back when we is done

Mr Hansen picks up the jar and wraps it in the handkerchief.
He bangs the whole lot down on the table.
He blows on it.
Then he opens the handkerchief to reveal a new, differently coloured intact egg again. He gives her the egg.

Mill
As it is
Would you be seeing that Bill if I wasn't here showing

it to you? Look at it.
Would you now?

She shows it to Bill.

Mill

Is a new H'egg

She passes it around.
They look with some wonder at Mr Hansen.

A new H'egg. Feel like is just been laid.
How is that happening?
Where is the jar gone?

Mr Hansen

Same place as the egg went

Mill once again looks all through the handkerchief.

Mill

Bet you couldn't be doing it a third time

Bill

Mill, Mr Hansen is our guest

Mill

Third time, is the thing.
Yous may been doing it once, twice, but could you be doing it for a third time?
Once more
Once more and I won't be going asking you favours again. After all you's gone and made our H'eggshell disappear and then given us a jar and then that is gone again now

Mr Hansen

You have a new egg

Mill

I was liking more the jar

Mr Hansen

You can't bargain with magic

She hands the handkerchief back.

Mill
Once more

Mr Hansen
Then I must go
Agreed?

She nods.

Mr Hansen
Give me the egg

Mill doesn't want to part with it.

Mr Hansen
The egg or I can't do it

She gives him the egg.

Mr Hansen
I'll tell you a story first
It's a story about a jar
The first time I saw a jar I was four years old
Standing in front of a sweet shop
Most children would have been looking at the sweets
But I was looking at the jars
A brown glass jar with a lid
And behind it another
Rows and rows of them, little ones, big ones
Jars with screw lids, cork lids, without any lids at all
And from that moment I knew
I was hooked
The rest of my life I was going to spend buying them,
selling them,
Making them
It might sound simple to you Mrs Lavarello
But jars are my life

*Once again he puts the egg in the handkerchief, bangs it
on the table, then blows on it.*

He pauses, holding the effect.
They are all intent on what it will have become,
although when Mr Hansen catches Bill's eye, Bill
pretends not to be interested.
He opens the handkerchief to reveal a handful of coins.
He puts the coins into Mill's hands. Mill is enchanted.
Bill jumps up.

Bill

Put them away

Mill

Sit down Bill

Bill

We aren't be wanting them. Give them back Mill,
here be giving them back to Mr Hansen

Mill

He gave them to me

Bill tries to snatch them.

Bill

Mill

Mill

No

Bill

They belongs to Mr Hansen

Mill

I's the one holding them

Bill

They is coming from inside of his handkerchief

Mill

They is coming from the second H'egg, which is
coming from the jar which is coming from my
H'eggshell.

Mr Hansen

My eggshell

Mill pauses and looks at Mr Hansen.

Mr Hansen

You gave the egg to me.
It was my eggshell.
My jar, my second egg and my coins.

He takes the coins back from Mill.
Mill looks bemused.
Mr Hansen stands up.

Mr Hansen

Good evening to you all

Mr Hansen walks out.
There is a short silence after he has gone.

Mill

Now see what you is done
Bill, he is taken my coins
I is never had coins before

Mill runs to the door and watches him go.
Francis starts to leave.

Bill

Wait you

Francis

Why?

Bill

What is he about?
What is he doing?

Francis

What?

Bill

Here?
Why is he come here?

Francis looks perplexed. He starts to speak then changes his mind.

Bill

Be telling me I'm wrong
Francis
Be telling me he isn't here to bring his business
Be telling me that Francis
That you and he . . .

Francis

Is a surprise.

Bill

No

Francis

He told me not to tell you yet

Pause.

Francis

Yes
Is a factory
A factory Aunty Mill
Right here on the island

Bill

No Francis, can't be
We is got nothing
What is we got that he could be wanting?

Francis

Crawfish
Crawfish
Crawfish from our island
To put in his jars

At dusk the same day. By the shore.
Rebecca is bathing in the sea.
Francis is sitting by the water's edge, facing away from
her and playing with some rocks.
Rebecca climbs out of the water behind him. She is
naked and pregnant.

Francis
Is nowhere has sand like this
Nowhere
Is nowhere as light
As shiny
As black

Francis throws them down.

Francis
I looked for you as I stepped off the boat

Rebecca picks up a towel.

Francis
And in the village
I looked for you all over.

Rebecca starts drying herself.

Francis
I came around to your house this afternoon
I walked up and down
Everywhere

Rebecca
Stop

Francis
Have you missed me?
Missed me missed me?
I thought about you

All the time
What you were doing, what you were thinking

Rebecca
Be turning
Francis be turning around
Look at me

Francis does so.
He sees her pregnant stomach for the first time.
Pause.
Rebecca starts to put on her clothes.

Rebecca
I was telling you not to go
Time and time I was telling you
Stay with me I was saying
Stay with me
Don't go
I know, you don't need to be telling me again
I was hearing it at the time
You was needing to go
That's what you said
You was needing to go

Rebecca laughs.

Rebecca
You was needing to go
Like the reading and numbers and all those things
you was needing to do
Needing to
Well you is been now. Isn't you?

She picks up her stuff and starts to walks away.

Francis
They hated me
Rebecca?
They hated me
Everywhere I went they . . .

They said I talked funny
I dressed like . . .
I didn't know what CUNT meant
Do you know what CUNT is meaning?
They played a trick on me
Pretended they were my friend then . . .
The men I was working with they . . .
And every time I did something or said something
In my stupid island way of talking . . .
I kept a piece of glass in my pocket
Here against my leg
A broken piece of a jar
That could cut deep.
And every time I got it wrong or forgot
I turned it
Further and further in.

Rebecca
    Francis . . .

Rebecca is more gentle now.

Francis
    Do you know what CUNT means Rebecca?
    Oh yes, of course you know
    Of course you do
    CUNT and SCREW and FUCK and all those words
    You know all about it

Rebecca starts to walk off.
Francis calls after her.

Francis
    I love you

Then more quietly after she is gone.

Francis
    I love you

The middle of the same night. Mill and Bill's house.
Bill is having a sleepless night and is fully dressed in his
outdoor clothes.
He stands in the kitchen, surrounded by three large sacks
of potatoes.
He empties the sacks onto the floor, and starts dividing
the potatoes one by one into seven smaller piles,
muttering seven surnames as he goes (Rodgers, Repetto,
Hagan, Glass, Green, Lavarello, Swain).
Mill comes down in her night dress.
She watches him without saying anything. Then:

Mill
  Bill?

Bill
  Back to bed

Mill
  They's the seeding 'tatoes

Bill carries on muttering.

Mill
  Who is these piles for?

Bill
  Back to bed with you

Mill
  Bill?
  You is giving away our crop?

Bill
  Tch woman

Mill
  What?

Bill

You is made me lose count

He goes around the piles adding one as he passes. Mill comes and gets in his way.

Bill

Away with you Mill

Mill

Not till you tells me

Bill

You wouldn't be understanding

Mill

I's might
Yous been odd all evening Bill. What's got into you?
Come away back to bed now love

Bill

No

Mill

Bill?

Bill

This is important
Is wanting to stay do this

Mill

But what is you doing?

Bill

I's making my will

Pause.

Mill

What?

Bill stops and considers.
He decides to say something, then changes his mind.
He puts another couple of potatoes down.

Bill

I is wanting to be ready

Mill

For what?

Bill looks at her.

Bill

For whatever.

Mill sits on the big central pile and protects them, so he can't reach.

Bill

Out of the way

Mill

Answer me why?
Is my potatoes too

Bill

I is dug them

Mill

We's married Bill

Bill

I's leaving you the biggest share

Mill

I's not wanting any

Bill

Out the way then

Mill

Answer me why?
I's not moving until you is telling me

Bill stops for a second.

Bill

Is all bad Mill
I don't like it

Mill

Tch

Bill

They is told me

Mill

Who?

Bill

The Old Hands

Mill

What?

Bill

Is when they is saved me. Before when I is drowning
because the water is juddering.
They is come and pull me out.
Watch out for the water
Watch out for the water, they is saying
The water is turning

Mill

They is actually speaking. You is sure?

Bill

The water is turning
Watch out for the water
Over and over
And the water is turning, all around

Mill

Tch

Bill

Harry was there

Mill

He was not

Bill

Harry Repetto. Plain as I is seeing you now.

Mill

No

Bill

Still has half the church roof with him
You go up there and see for yourself Mill, then you
will be believing me

Mill

The only thing turning is you William Lavarello
Is turning soft in the head

Pause.

Mill

Is madness Bill
What about me? Should I be making my will?

Bill

Maybe
Don't know but maybe

Mill

Tch

Bill

Don't say I didn't warn you when is happening

Mill

When what is happening?

Bill

I don't know
Is just it. I don't know
Move out the way, let me get on
I is only known the water go like this once before Mill

Pause.

Mill

You is always been the sensible one
You is the one that is always told me not to pay any

heed to this or to that
Don't be getting any ideas you is always saying

Bill starts dividing his potatoes again.

Bill
I's leaving you the house

Mill
Is too kind

Bill
Is nothing

Mill
Bill . . . stop this
You is scaring me

Bill
I's just being prepared Mill

Mill
Please . . .
Please stop Bill

She puts her hands over her ears.

Mill
Ok, say I is believing you, and I isn't saying I is,
but say I is and I is going up the water's edge and
is seeing what you seen, and say you is right all the
Old Hands is there, and say they is all saying things

Bill
And the water is gone juddery

Mill
And the water is gone juddery

Bill
Turning over and over. Round and round

Mill
Turning over and over. Round and round

So?
You isn't needing to take it to heart
You takes it to heart too much Bill

Bill

What?

Mill

Might be they is scaring you
Is having a game
Is only a bunch of shadows
The Old Hands? The Old Hands is all dead

Bill

You can't be saying that Mill

Mill

Why not?
What do they know?
Harry Repetto was always talking like the birds is
shitting anyway
Only is God knows anything
You could decide you is paying them no heed
Ignore it
Might be they is wrong anyway
Is made a mistake
Is having a game
Is making you see things
Is making the water shake, so what?

Bill

Was like the time before

Mill

Come on Bill
You and me is going to make old bones.
Old old bones
We is going to be living in this little house of ours,
with our 'tatoes and our patches until we is one
hundred and ten.

One hundred and ten
Is no need to be making a will for a long while yet
Remember what we is used to saying when we was
young?

Bill nods reluctantly.

Mill

So is all alright then.

Mill comes and puts an arm around him.

Mill

We is going to be alright
We is all going to be just fine

Bill looks at the piles of potatoes.
Mill starts picking them up and putting them back into
the bag they came from.

Bill

I isn't so certain Mill

Mill

What?

Bill

Was seeing them so clearly, and the water

Mill

Bill?

Bill

Maybe I is safer making the will, then getting a
surprise if I isn't needing it just yet

Mill

Bill?

Mill is starting to lose her patience.

Mill

You isn't even trying here
Could you be at least trying?

Bill

You is giving in to it, that is what you is doing. You
was easy bait for them old hands, and as for that
Harry Repetto, if he isn't died already I is wanting
to kill him myself. What is he thinking, scaring an
old man like you?
Tomorrow is a Sunday Bill
We is having to go to bed

Bill

I wish Francis hadn't gone to Cape Town

Mill

Is nothing to do with Francis

Bill

Only like this one time before.
Only like this once.

Francis walks in.
Silence.
He sits down at the table.

Mill

You is coming back up Bill?
We can be talking in the morning
Sleep
Is making you feel better
And tomorrow is a Sunday

Mill goes to Francis and gives him a kiss.

Mill

Is lovely to have you back love
You is needing to be taking care of this uncle you is got
His mind be playing tricks again

Mill leaves.
Bill is awkward in front of Francis.
He isn't sure now whether to carry on with his will or not.

He brings over a pile of potatoes and puts them down in front of Francis.

Bill
You look after them well
They is good ones
And is a patch
Is your name on it

Francis
Why?

Bill shrugs.
Francis indicates the piles of potatoes on the floor.

Francis
What is all this for?

Bill starts putting the potatoes away.

Bill
Up to bed lad

Francis
No

Bill
You is tired

Pause.

Francis
I couldn't sleep tonight

Bill
Shut your eyes and be listening to the wind then

Francis
I need to think

Bill
Bed is the best place for it.

Pause.
Bill continues putting the potatoes away.

Francis
Did you know about Rebecca?

Beat.

Bill
Yes

Francis
You didn't tell me

Beat.

Francis
Never mind

Bill
We wasn't sure . . .

Pause.

Francis
Expect everyone blames me
Is that right?
Is that what they are saying?
What did I expect, going off to Cape Town?
Leaving her by herself?
That is what they are saying, isn't it Uncle Bill?

Bill doesn't answer.

Francis
To think I missed you all
Even you
I even missed you.

Pause.

Bill
Is no one blaming you

Francis fiddles with the plates on the table.

Francis
Anyway she'll be sorry

One day when she sees
She'll be sorry

Pause.
Bill can't decide whether to say anything or not, finally
blurts out:

Bill
Be careful with this Mr Hansen, Francis
You need to be careful
So you met him in Cape Town, doesn't mean you
knows him

Pause.

Bill
Does it?
We isn't knowing anything about him
He could be anyone

He turns around to look at Francis.

Bill
Oh I knows he's very clever
I isn't denying that
But I isn't so sure about him
I isn't trusting him
Come here and do fancy magic
So what? Is meaning nothing
Is not so good
Isn't magic
Is a trick
And is you he's tricking
This factory idea is . . .
Is no good Francis
Is no good

Francis
You don't even know what it would be like
You haven't even heard the plans

Bill

I is heard enough
I is seen enough

Francis

We is both seen

Beat.

Bill

What I is seen is in Mr Hansen's face
Right here between the eyes
I isn't liking it
Our island crawfish
And he is thinking money
We isn't wanting that
Our crawfish for Mr Hansen's money

Francis

Be something new
Be something to do

Bill

We isn't wanting something new

Francis

We isn't or you isn't?

Beat.

Bill

We isn't

Francis

NO
You isn't
They'll be saying yes
They'll be loving it
It's you
Is you that is frightened

Beat.

Bill

Is nothing wrong with being frightened Francis
We isn't like Cape Town here

Francis

Anyway it isn't up to you
You is just given me a patch

Bill

Still will be needing to go to the vote
Everyone is having a say

Francis

So is up to everyone

Bill

Everyone? Yes,
After everyone has asked everyone what they is
thinking
And this everyone is asked that everyone
And that everyone is asked the next everyone
And the next and the next
Until no one is made up their minds, Francis.
They is all just watching see what everyone else is
doing,
Then someone is looking at me.
What is Bill saying, they is asking?
What is Bill saying?
And then they is all asking what is Bill saying?
What is Bill saying? What is Bill saying?
And maybe if I could be saying Yes, and meaning Yes
Then everyone is saying Yes,
The Yes and we is having this factory
But
If I is saying No
And meaning No . . .

Beat.

Francis

No one tried to stop you
Twenty years ago, no one tried to stop you
When you came back from Cape Town and had this
great idea
Build a church
No one said anything
You didn't have to go to the vote
Ask everyone if they wanted it
You just went straight in and did it

Bill

Was different then
We needed it

Francis

Took everyone up to the lake
Baptised the whole island in a single day
No questions then

Bill

We was needing it

Francis

Taught us things, read us things, told us stories, all
those stories, on Sundays about the bible
Did you ask any of us?

Beat.

Bill

Is you ever seen a dog eat a man Francis?
Seen bodies is strewn like . . .
Of course you isn't
I is glad you isn't
But I is seen it
H'out there
H'outside
When I was there
They was having a name for it

They was saying there is reasons
Complicated reasons
Is war they is called it
Was country against country
Is to do with armies
But it was dogs. Dogs chewing dead mens
But whatever has been done out there
I is seen just as bad done here
Oh maybe is not bodies strewn
And maybe is not dogs
Maybe is not war
But is as bad

Pause.

We was needing a church but we isn't needing a
factory.

Francis
I don't believe you
Dogs don't eat men

Bill
I saw them

Francis
No
You are just saying this to stop me

Bill
No, I isn't wanting to stop you
Just is wanting you to be thinking

Beat.

Bill
What will the factory be bringing?
What do we need, that we isn't got?
Here we is working for ourselves
You is wanting us all to be working for Mr Hansen
for the rest of our days?

Francis

Is better than just being stuck with the mountain and
the patches

Beat.

Bill

Alright

Bill comes and sits next to Francis

Bill

Alright Francis
Take it to the vote
Tell them about your idea
Be letting them make up their minds
Be doing and saying what you want to persuade them
I won't be saying a thing
Neither way
Not a word.
You can be taking it to the vote and I won't even be
raising my hand

Pause

Bill

If you is doing something for me
If.
Is only on condition you is doing this thing
Isn't for me, is for you,
Is for all of us
Is just a little thing
Be going up to the mountain first thing in the morning
Be standing at the pool
Be washing yourself in the water, Francis
Walking right in until is up to your waist
Be putting your head down under the surface
And listen
Just be listening
Is all

You listen
You see what you can hear
Then you'll be knowing whether is right or not
You decide

Pause.

Bill

Is up to you lad
Is all up to you now
I is going to bed

Bill walks up the stairs.

SCENE FIVE

The following morning.
Rebecca is sitting by herself on a patch of land,
overlooking the sea.
Mill and Mr Hansen arrive. Mill sits down a little
distance away from Rebecca.

Mill

Be running along Rebecca.

Rebecca doesn't move.

Mill

Be running along, we is sitting here

Rebecca

I is sitting here

Mill

And so is we
You can be sitting somewhere else now
Go on
We is busy here
Be sitting Mr Hansen

Mill pats the ground beside her.
Mr Hansen sits.
Rebecca doesn't move.

Mill
Said move
We is waiting on something important

Rebecca
So is I

Mill
What is you waiting on?

Rebecca
The sea

Mill
The sea is always here
Along with you girl
You be waiting for the sea someplace farther along
Or go and be smiling at the sailors on the boat, why
don't you?
Go and be smiling at the sailors like you is done before

Rebecca
I is never smiled at no sailors
NEVER.

Rebecca moves off.

Rebecca
NEVER NEVER

Mill watches her go, then says to Mr Hansen after she is gone:

Mill
Well is must have been smiling at someone

Mr Hansen is nervous, he is tapping his foot on the ground.

Mill
They won't be long

Mr Hansen
They've been hours

Mill
They'll be out soon
When is the boat be leaving?

Mr Hansen
Tomorrow

Mill
They'll be out by then

Pause.

Mill
Be telling me again

Mr Hansen
What?

Mill
I likes hearing

Mr Hansen
No, my mind's busy

Mr Hansen paces up and down a bit.

Mill
Change your mind of it

Mr Hansen sits down with a sigh. He gets a jar out of his pocket.

Mr Hansen
I don't know where to begin

Mill
With the machines,
Machines you and Francis is going to build

Mr Hansen stands up, he takes a few steps.

Mr Hansen
The machines will go about here

Mill
Here or here?

Mr Hansen
There

Mill
How many?

Mr Hansen
Five to begin with

Mill
Then maybe six

Mr Hansen
Then maybe six

Mill
What will they be looking like?

Mr Hansen
Big

Mill
And delicate
With great long knives

Mr Hansen
Like great . . .

Mill
Flapping birds
And where is I going to be?

Mr Hansen
You'll be here
Some of you. Standing along here

Mill
Dressing like this?

Mr Hansen

No, wearing uniform

Mill

Is wearing my H'uniform
You's forgetting the buttons

Mr Hansen

Each of you will have a panel in front of you

Mill

With buttons

Mr Hansen

With buttons

Mill

And when we is pressing the buttons, the machine
goes . . .

Mr Hansen

It comes on

*Mill switches the imaginary button and the imaginary
machine comes on.*

Mill

Goes brrr
But what is here?

Mr Hansen

Here will be the engine room

Mill

Is needing the H'engine to be firing the machines
Is the H'engine men that is working in the H'engine
room
But we is forgotten the jar-ing room
Be telling me about the jar-ing room

Mr Hansen

You tell me

Mill

No, you do the saying

Mr Hansen

You know as well as I do.

Mill

I want you to be saying.

Mr Hansen

Well when the chopped crayfish go out of the
machines, which they do about here . . .

Mill

Or here, is depending whether we is having five or
six . . .

Mr Hansen

They'll be carried along.

Mill

On this thing, is like a belt but isn't a belt, is much
bigger, and moving, and will go right the way along,
right here.

Mr Hansen

Until . . .

Mill

Poof.

Mr Hansen

Comes out here.

Mill

In the jar-ing room,
Where we is all standing in a line.

Mr Hansen

And will put the pieces into the jars.

Mill

Only not any-old-how, but carefully so is same

amount in each.
But where is Francis?

Mr Hansen
Francis?

Mill
He's being the controller.

Mr Hansen
Then he's in the controller's room.

Mill
With the glass window?

Mr Hansen
A glass window so he can watch the machines.

Mill
And us.

Mr Hansen
And you.

Mill
And if we is doing something wrong?

Mr Hansen
He'll tap on the glass.

Mill
And when the bell is going?

Mr Hansen
You'll stop.

Mill
Be turning the machines off first.

Mr Hansen
Of course.

Mill
Pushing the buttons, say stop, the machine is going . . .
nothing

Is stopped
Then we is taking off the H'uniform, is walking along
here . . . .
To here
Here is where we is sitting
Eating our lunch

Mr Hansen
We'll build a canteen for you

Mill
Canteen?

Mr Hansen
A place to eat lunch

Mill
We'll be sitting in our canteen
And the name of the factory is saying 'Mr Hansen
and Francis'

Mr Hansen
Just Hansen

Mill
What about Francis?

Mr Hansen
He'll have his name inside

Mill
On his desk?

Mr Hansen
Yes

Mill
Behind the glass?

Mr Hansen
Yes

Mill
In the controller's room?

Mr Hansen
Yes

Mill
Say 'Francis Swain,
Controller'

She mimes this.
Mr Hansen sits down.

Mill
You can't be sitting down, you has to do the talking

Mr Hansen
You've said it all

Mill
No I hasn't. You be saying more

Mr Hansen
I'm tired

Mill
I'm tired
I's been filling all the jars

Mr Hansen
Come and sit down then

Mill
In the canteen?

Mr Hansen
Yes

Mill sits down in the canteen.

Mill
I is made you a cup of tea if you want one

Mr Hansen
Thank you

Mill
Come and drink it then

Mr Hansen goes over and sits beside her.
She gives him a mimed cup. He takes it and nearly
drinks but then comes to his senses.
He very quickly becomes anxious again and looks
around.
Mill is more interested in her mimed tea and the whole
factory fantasy.
Then she notices his anxiety.

Mill
They'll be along soon

Mr Hansen gets up again and looks at his watch.

Mill
Drink your tea, it'll be getting cold
You know I is thinking the canteen be better over the
other side

He looks at her.

Mill
Be getting a better view of the sea is all

Mr Hansen
Here they come

Mr Hansen jumps up.
Mill finishes her mimed cup of tea and stays where she is
at first.
Francis and Bill walk back.
Neither man says anything.

Mr Hansen
Well, go on.

Pause.

Bill

Is off

Over

Mr Hansen

What?

Francis

Is right

Mr Hansen

They voted it out?

Bill

No

They voted it in

They loved the idea

Mr Hansen

I don't understand

Francis

I voted it out

Mr Hansen

Why?

Francis?

Francis

I'm sorry

Mr Hansen

I don't understand

Bill

Is needing to be getting back to your other concerns
now I suppose Mr Hansen

Mr Hansen

I need an explanation

Mill

What is going on here?

Mill leaves her tea and comes over.

Bill

There isn't going to be any factory

Mill

Why not?

Bill

Francis is changed his mind

Mill

Can he be doing that?

Bill

Is done

Mill

What about the canteen and the H'uniform?

Bill

What canteen and H'uniform?

Mill

He was going to build us a canteen to go in the factory
And the H'uniform

Francis

I'm sorry Mr Hansen

Mr Hansen

You said there would be no problem

Bill

They'll be no canteen now

Francis

I didn't think there would be . . . I,

Mill

No H'uniform?

Bill

No H'uniform

Mr Hansen
I came all this way

Francis
I know

Bill
Come on Mill
They is needing to talk

Mill
Don't stand there, you is standing on the controller's room

Francis
Here,
I'm sorry

Francis gives Mr Hansen back the briefcase.

Mr Hansen
What, so that is it?
Final?
Over?
No more discussion?
Do you know how many miles I have travelled Francis?
How much time I have put into this?
How much . . .
God I was a fool to have ever even thought
Look at you, you're a kid, a lad
Just a lad
To even have met you was
Alright
So it is over
Finis
Gone
End of a dream
Island crayfish, no longer
But what about my time?
Time is money Francis?

What about all the money I spent?
You can't do this to people
Not without an explantion
You just changed your mind?
That's crap
Sorry Mrs Lavarello, but it's crap

Bill

You can be telling him more than that, can't you?
Be telling him what you saw

Mill

What?

Bill

He is heard something
Is heard something in the water Mr Hansen
Is gone to the lake Mill
Early this morning is what he is said
Francis?

Mr Hansen

Enough is enough
He heard something?
This I don't believe

Bill

Tell him Francis
Yes, in the water

Mr Hansen

No.
Sorry
I've had it
I'm not interested any more
I've changed my mind
I don't want to hear
This is business Mr Lavarello, not some . . .
I don't care what he heard or saw
I'm going back to the ship

Francis
I'm sorry Mr Hansen

Mr Hansen looks about the island. He sniffs the air.

Mr Hansen
No
I'm the sorry one
It is still a beautiful island

He gives the briefcase to Mill.

Mr Hansen
You keep this.
Who knows?
Maybe you'll need it some day

He takes a jar out of his pocket and gives it to Francis.

Mr Hansen
And you
See if you can turn it back into an egg

Bill
We have plenty H'eggs

Mr Hansen
Use it to store them in then

Mr Hansen leaves.
Francis sits down heavily. He looks at the jar.

Bill
Is right you is a lad, but you is a good lad

Mill
Francis?

Francis doesn't respond, he looks at Mill.

Francis
When I was in Cape Town he was my only friend.

Bill
Be standing up lad

You is done a good thing
Is so proud of you, is so proud
Is really good to be having you home
Isn't it Mill?
Is really good to be having him home

Mill

Is all in favour yesterday
Is thinking is a good idea

Bill

That was yesterday wasn't it Francis?

Mill

Is you really seen the water Francis?

Francis

I is sorry Mill

Bill

Is no reason to be sorry
Is done a good thing, is no reason to be sorry

Mill

Is you really seen it?

Pause.

Bill

Of course he is seen it
Isn't you lad?
Anyone be seeing it if they went up there
You be telling her Francis

Mill

Francis?

Bill

Is shaking Mill, like is done before

Francis

NO.

Stop Uncle Bill
Is nothing shaking

Bill

But you said you saw . . .

Francis

I didn't see anything
If I is said I did, I is said it to shut you up is all.

Bill

You is lying
He is lying Mill, don't listen
Is lying

Mill

Hush now Bill

Bill

NO.
Tell her.
Be telling her the truth

Francis

You're trapped, Uncle Bill
It is all mixed up in your mind
You is built your church,
You is made the island the way you want
But now it is trapping you

Pause.

Francis

I'm sorry Aunty Mill
But I is made a decision
Was a mistake to think I could be living here again
Here?
I don't know what I was thinking
I'm going to go back to Cape Town with Mr Hansen

Pause.

Francis

I'll leave with the boat.

Mill

Francis, no?

Francis

There is nothing for me here any more Aunty Mill

Francis looks from one to another.

Francis

I had better get my stuff together,
Catch Mr Hansen.
I . . .
Aunty Mill?
I am not a lad.

He puts the jar that Mr Hansen gave him down into the sand.

Mill

Francis . . .?

Francis walks away, leaving Bill and Mill in silence.

Mill

Go after him Bill.

Bill doesn't move.

Mill

Go after him

Bill

He did see . . .

Mill

No, Bill
Not one more word
We is always losing everything
Everything is always being taken away from us
Not Francis

Francis is all that we ever had
Go after him
Change his mind of it
Quick

Pause.

Bill

It wasn't just the wind. He did hear . . .

Mill

BILL

Pause.

Why is you not going after him? Oh, yes, I is
forgetting, you is never cared for Francis. Just
be standing back watching him go. Say 'Goodbye
Francis – on you go'? As easy as that, because is
Swain. Isn't Lavarello so you is pleased to see
him go.

Bill

Isn't true Mill.
His mind is made is all.
Won't be anything I can be saying to change it

Mill

Well maybe you is going to watch him go
But I isn't
No.
I is had enough

Bill

What is you meaning?

Mill

If Francis is leaving
He's not the only one on that boat be waving you
goodbye

Beat.

73

Mill

Francis is leaving this island tomorrow and I'll be leaving with him

Beat.

Bill

NO
No Mill
Don't say that.
You isn't knowing what you are saying

Mill

I is knowing Bill
Francis goes and I go

Bill

But . . .
You and me, we is . . .
You can't be going Mill

Mill

Why not?

Bill

Is the H'outside World Mill.
Is . . .

Mill

Is the H'outside World is all
If Francis be managing then so is I.
Mr Hansen been telling me about all these new things
I isn't going to stay here with just you and the patches
Not without Francis

Bill

NO.

Mill

You had better be minding me.

Bill

Is no way I can be making him stay Mill
He is never listening to me

Mill

Then tomorrow you and I is saying goodbye.

Bill

Is you and me here, is our lives here
Is Old Bones, Mill?

Mill

Not without Francis
Is no life here without Francis

Bill

Mill?

Mill

I is meaning it Bill.
Francis goes and I go.

She stands up. She brushes the mud off her skirt and leaves.

SCENE SIX

The same day. Rebecca's house.
Bill arrives at Rebecca's front door. Rebecca answers it.

Rebecca

Oh.

Bill

Can I come in?

Rebecca

Is no one here

Bill

Is you I is come to see

Rebecca
Me?

She opens the door. Bill walks in and sits down at the table.

Rebecca
If Francis is sent you I is not interested in hearing

Bill
Francis isn't sent me

Rebecca
Oh.

Pause.
Rebecca looks about her.

Rebecca
Is no tea.
No milk
Cow is on strike
Isn't eating
Isn't moving
Is giving no milk for four days
So don't be asking me for tea

Rebecca sits.
She is trying her best to be polite.

Rebecca
If you want water I can be taking it from the stream

Bill
No
No water.

Pause.

Rebecca
So, what is you wanting?

Bill doesn't answer.

Is you sure you is come to see me?
No one is ever come to see me.

Bill
Francis is leaving

Rebecca doesn't answer.

Bill
Tomorrow
Is leaving with the boat

Pause.

Bill
Has you heard?

Rebecca nods.

Rebecca
Why?

Bill
Lots of reasons
And you
You and lots of reasons

Pause.

Rebecca
Francis is never doing anything because of me

Pause.

Bill
Is never coming back
You know that?
Not never
He goes and none of us is ever seeing him again

Rebecca
Francis makes up his own mind
Doesn't listen to no one else

Bill

Francis has always had a mind that could make itself
up
But is not only Francis
Milly
Is saying she will be going too
My Milly
Is saying she is going where Francis goes
Oh and she is meaning it
Is all ready to be stepping on that boat, wave me off
as it disappears
And once Mill is leaving then the next person be
leaving
And then the next is leaving
And then the next and the next . . .

Rebecca

Mr Lavarello,
Is nothing to do with me.

She stands up.

Bill

Say the child is his

Pause.
Then a second pause as Rebecca realises that Bill
means it.

Rebecca

Is a lie

Bill

I know

Rebecca

You is asking me to lie?
You?

Bill shrugs.
Pause.

Rebecca
Is impossible anyway

Bill
Impossible?

Rebecca
Impossible Francis is the father

Bill
Impossible or unlikely?

Rebecca
Impossible

Pause.

Rebecca
Unless you isn't counting right

Bill
Francis isn't able to count

Rebecca
Yes he is

Bill
Not very well

Rebecca
Francis is able to count very well indeed

Bill
But he won't

Rebecca
He might

Bill
Be taking the risk, Rebecca
Please

Pause.
Rebecca has a hard look at Bill.

Rebecca

You always was telling us lies is wrong

Bill

I know

Rebecca

All my life you is telling us . . .

Bill

I know

Pause.

Rebecca

No
I isn't going to
I couldn't be doing it
Not for ever
For ever and ever

Bill

He is wanting it to be
Very badly
He would stay and . . .
You and he . . .

Rebecca

No no no
Stop saying this

Bill

Has you already told the someone else?

Rebecca

No

Bill

So why is you crying?

Pause.
Bill stands up.

Bill
I is sorry I has troubled you

Bill starts to leave.

Bill
I'll see you tomorrow
At the shore

Beat.

Bill
You are a good girl Rebecca

Rebecca
No
I is not
I's bad
You don't know me.
I's bad.
Very very bad

Bill
I should not be troubling you

Rebecca
I isn't wanting Francis to leave

Bill
I know

Rebecca
Don't be going just yet
Be . . .
Be letting me think
Be letting me . . .
I can't, I . . .
If I said yes,
If I was saying yes
Is only if
If I is saying yes, what would you do?
Would you be doing anything?

Would you be surprised?
Is you thinking I won't?
Definitely
Because I might,
I might just
I might
If I did, what would you be doing?

Bill
Cry
Just for joy
Francis be staying and my Mill

Rebecca
Is nothing
Crying
Anyone can cry
I can cry
I can cry by myself
Don't need to say lies to cry

Beat.

Rebecca
What else would you be doing?

Beat.

Bill
What is you wanting?

Rebecca laughs.

Rebecca
No
Not what I is wanting
Is what you is wanting
Nobody is caring what I want
Nobody is even knowing what I want

Bill
What do you want?

Rebecca

I want this baby dead

Beat.

Rebecca

There, I is said it
I is wanting this baby dead
The second this baby is born
As soon as it is breathing
The very second, I want someone to be picking it up,
Like this and turning it round and holding it down,
Hard, its face in the sand,
And to keep holding and holding it down so hard.
Until . . .

Pause.

Bill

Rebecca . . . I

Rebecca

See I is told you I is bad
Bad bad.

Bill

You is wanting someone to kill your child?

Rebecca

Is not my child
I is just the carrier
I's just like a ship is carrying it

Pause.

Rebecca

I know
I know you is saying that you can't
You can't
Of course you can't
Is obvious you can't

Beat.

Rebecca
But I is thinking you could
Just
Just for a minute, maybe, you could
That was all
If you was wanting to badly enough
And I know you is wanting me to say yes very bad
I was thinking that maybe, you could
You could maybe . . .
Could you?

SCENE SEVEN

Bill by the water.
He should not move to the water but be suddenly
surrounded by it.
He is up to his waist again, and the deafening juddering
is all around.
He shouts out 'What are you?'
Silence.

SCENE EIGHT

A few days later.
Mill and Francis, inside Mill's house.
It is exactly the same as the start of the Act, apart from
a cloth on the table, and a general feeling that it has
been prettied.
Francis has just entered.
Mill is calm.

Mill
Been waiting
Since the sun is first up

Been watching through the chinks in the roof as up
it came
Been holding my breath as the hours go by

Francis
Mill . . .

Mill
Don't touch me
Stay where you are
I's wanting to see you first
Other way
You'll not be coming back to visit I suppose now
You'll be like a stranger to the pair of us

Francis
No

Mill
Oh you may be as thinking you won't but you isn't
knowing
You'll be getting busy and forgetting all about us
Won't you?
You won't will you Francis?

Francis
I'll be less than a mile.

Mill
Ah but I is remembering my mother saying this to
my sister and she is saying 'No' but ding, the day
she is marrying that is it, she is only coming back
for Christmases and one Sunday a month and she
is only living up the stairs.

Francis
I'll be coming back to visit

Mill
And then is the baby
You won't be having time when the baby is come

Should have been telling me it was your baby Francis,
All these months of seeing Rebecca be growing and
was your baby
Be turning again
Turning and turning
Is suiting you this suit
Is worn by my father, and your father
You is knowing that?
And Uncle Bill the day we is got wed
All of them is wearing this
And I is worn the wedding dress Rebecca be wearing
We is all worn it
Oh sure, never be the same again now Rebecca is
worn it, is had to put three extra pieces up the side,
but still . . .
I is told her is she sure she is only having one baby
Maybe you is best standing on your toes because
those trousers is far too long at the bottom

Francis stands up on his toes.

Mill
Is much better

Francis
Bill isn't even spoke to me

Mill
He doesn't mean it
You know what he is like
Be giving him time

Francis drops down again.

Mill
No, be staying like that
You must be staying like that Francis
Have you got a flower?

Francis
No

Mill

Well why not?

Is the whole of the island to be getting a flower from

Francis

Not at this time of year

Mill

Must be having a flower Francis

Can't be getting married without a flower

They all had flowers, every one of them, my mother was seeing to that

Francis

It doesn't matter Mill

Mill

Maybe is not mattering to you Francis but is mattering to me

Francis

We can't get one now, there is no way

Mill

Mr Hansen could

Francis

Aunty Mill

Mill

What?

He'd make us a flower as soon as look at us

Just be crushing a leaf in his hankie and ding . . .

beautiful flower.

Francis

Don't

Mill

Why not?

Francis

I don't like to hear his name

Mill

Nonsense

Francis

It makes me feel bad inside

Mill

Is being silly.
Mr Hansen is a friend of yours

Francis

No

Mill

Yes, I is seen the way you is coming in the door with him,
'Here is a friend of mine' you is saying

Francis

We isn't friends now

Mill

Is all over Francis
Mr Hansen is two days gone
Be over the horizon by now
Anyway we was making him feel welcome wasn't we?
But is no Mr Hansen here so is no flowers

Mill starts to look around the walls.

Mill

Is no flowers

Her eye catches on something on the walls.

Mill

Is not a flower I is agreeing but . . .

She takes down a magazine picture of a tree.

Mill

What is you saying to this?
Can be putting this in your lapel eh?

She goes to get some scissors and starts to cut it out.

Francis

I can't be wearing that

Mill

Why not?

Francis

Isn't anything like a flower

Mill

I know
Is better
There is plenty of flowers on the island when the
month is right
But never a tree
Now you wait a minute, you'll look fine

Francis

Mill?

Mill

No complaining Francis

*Mill busies herself with cutting out the tree, Francis
walks around.*

Francis

I saw everyone

Mill

Hmm?

Francis

Waiting
I didn't know you had told them all to wait

Mill

Where?

Francis

Out there, waiting for my wedding

Mill

I didn't tell them

Francis

Of course you did
They're all standing on the shore
In a long line

Mill

Nothing to do with me

Francis

They're not waiting for me?

Mill

No

Francis

They must be waiting for something

Mill

I suppose they must

Mill puts the tree in Francis' lapel.

Mill

Is looking lovely now
Rebecca won't be knowing you
When is she coming?

Francis

Soon
Actually is past the hour
Is a while ago she said she would be here.

Mill

Is taking her a while to walk now

Francis

I know but she said she would meet me here before

Mill

She'll be along

Francis

I know

Mill

Of course she'll be along
Is taking her time getting ready is all.
Maybe she is in the crowd

Francis

Why would she be in the crowd?

Mill

I don't know
Just an idea

Francis

Is her wedding day

Mill

I know

Francis

Why would she be standing in the crowd on her
wedding day?

Mill

I don't know

Francis

And why is the crowd standing out there anyway?
Waiting?
What is they waiting for?
The crowd is never standing outside like that on a
wedding day
Just looking
Should be standing in the church

Mill

Maybe is a boat coming

Francis

We is just had a boat

Mill

Or a storm
Was hearing thunder before

Francis

Maybe I will go up to her house
See where she is

Mill

Maybe she is forgotten the time
Is not so late
Few moments is all

Francis

I don't like them standing out there
Looking

Francis starts to go.

Mill

We'll be meeting you at the church, will we?
Be coming back here love, give me another kiss

Mill kisses Francis.

Mill

I is proud of you,
You know that?
Very proud.

Francis leaves.
Mill goes over and shouts up the stairs.

Mill

Bill?
Is you ready Bill?
Bill?
Is Francis' wedding day and you is supposed to be at
the church already

Bill comes down the stairs.

Bill

Is wonderful Mill
Is wonderful
Is so . . .

He takes her by the hands and swings her around.

Bill

I is been standing on the roof
Is beautiful and extraordinary
Come and be looking
Come come

Mill

You isn't even dressed

Bill

Isn't the water Mill
Isn't the water
And isn't my mind
Is the mountain underneath

Mill

What is you talking about?

Bill

I is seen it this morning
I is followed smoke up the mountain
Is great clouds of smoke
Coloured clouds, colours you is never seen
Pinks, reds, greens
And I is seen it
Is boiling now, is really boiling
Is coming up in bubbles of red red hot
So hot is burning your eyes to look at it
And steam and under the mountain is fire
Great arms of fire coming out, is like a little flower
with great arms
Go to the window Mill, be seeing for yourself
Quick

Mill

Bill?

Bill

Look Mill, be standing at the window
Was you ever seeing such a . . .

*Mill looks over to the window. She moves to have a
better view.*

Mill

Is hot?

Bill

Is so hot, would melt the moon

Mill looks again.

Mill

What about our houses?

Bill doesn't answer.

Mill

Don't want all those colours and fire and boiling
coming here

Bill shakes his head.

Bill

Is miles away
Is at the top of the mountain.
Is not coming here

Mill looks again.

Mill

You is sure?

Bill

I think it might be God, Mill

He gives her a kiss on both cheeks.

Bill

I think this might be God

After all this time . . .
I think this might be

Francis comes back in.

Mill
Where's Rebecca?

Francis
Is not coming
She . . . .
Is the baby
Her baby is started
She is screaming and crying
Our baby has started coming

Mill
Oh my Goodness

Francis
She is clutching herself here and saying she is ripping
apart

Mill
Who is with her?

Francis
No one

Mill
What?

Francis
I's frightened Mill

Mill
Wait a minute, I'll go

Francis
No. She doesn't want anyone

Mill
She may be saying that but . . .

Francis

She sent me away
She doesn't want anyone there
No one
She is saying that she wants to be alone
She is only asking for one person

Mill

Who?

Francis

Him.
You, Uncle Bill
She is asking for you.

The sound of juddering returns.
Bill picks up his jumper and walks out.
Mill and Francis watch him, motionless.
The juddering gets louder and with it is the sound of the
islanders' pandemonium and panic. A woman's piercing
scream is heard and this continues after the other sounds
have stopped.

SCENE NINE

On top of the screaming a pounding is heard.
Francis is pounding at the door of Rebecca's house, and
shouting her name.
He is half-hysterical and very weary. Eventually Mill
comes beside him.

Mill

Come on now Francis.
Come on.
Let's be going.

She leads him away.

SCENE TEN

The following dawn, with all its calm.
The immediate tremors from the mountain have stopped.
Rebecca is standing alone in her house.
She is wearing a slip and holding a wedding dress in her
arms. It is covered in blood.
In front of her is a bucket of water that she uses to try
and wash off the blood.
She stands up, and moves to a rocking chair and tries to
sit down.
All her movements are slow; she is very sore and also in
shock.
Bill enters. He stands beside her.
Neither of them say anything.
Rebecca starts to rock the chair very slowly.

Rebecca
Let's play a game the sailors said

Bill stands at her side, shattered.
Pause.

Rebecca
Come aboard, the sailors said

She rocks a little more.

Rebecca
Play a game
The sailors said

Bill
Was a girl

Rebecca
A game
Play . . .

Bill
   A tiny tiny little girl

Pause.
Rebecca hears this but doesn't show any reaction.

Rebecca
   Play a game they said
   A game

Pause.

Rebecca
   So I was playing, and they was playing
   On the big ship that was come
   Three of them
   And me
   Playing
   And laughing and laughing and
   Harder and harder
   Until I . . .
   Until I isn't wanting to . . .
   I isn't wanting to play any more
   And I is telling them stop
   Stop I is saying
   Stop stop
   Please stop
   But they's playing on
   And on
   And on
   And on
   Until . . .
   I . . .

Rebecca starts rocking again.
She forces herself to think of something else.
Bill lets out a long horrible howl that has welled up from
inside.
He crumples.

Rebecca doesn't know what to do but puts a hand on his
shoulders.
He moves in towards her and holds onto her legs,
desperate.
Rebecca doesn't move.

Bill
It was . . .

Rebecca
Shouldn't have ever even been . . .

Pause.

Rebecca
You must be . . .
Be standing
Is something is gone now
Is over
Is gone
Wasn't a baby
Was a thing should never have been born . . .

She helps him up.
He is more fragile than she is.

Bill
Saw something good today

Rebecca doesn't know what to say.

Bill
I . . .

He turns to her.

Bill
Was in the mountain
Was good, all good.

Bill suddenly realises.

Bill

Isn't baptised
Rebecca?
Is unbaptised
We can't . . .

Someone knocks impatiently three times on the door.
They both freeze.
Bill tries to turn around, confused.

Bill

Is no one born on the island that is unbaptised

More knocking.

Rebecca

Mr Lavarello
Stand up
Please
You is going to have to stand up

The knocking continues.

Rebecca

They is going to come in
We is going to have to let them in

Bill goes off to one of the other rooms.
Still more knocks.

Rebecca

What is you doing?
You . . .

Bill returns with the baby wrapped up in a blanket.
Rebecca looks on horrified.
Bill bends down and takes some of the water from the
bucket in his hand.
He unwraps the baby's head and baptises it.

Bill

In the name of the Father, Son and Holy Ghost I is
baptising you . . .

He looks at Rebecca.
Rebecca can hardly speak.

Rebecca

I isn't . . . .
Anything
Please
I isn't . . .
Misfortune

Bill

Misfortune.

He covers the head up again, very gently.

Bill

Misfortune

Pause
Again there is more knocking.
Pause
Bill holds onto the baby, and speaks so quietly he almost doesn't make a sound at all.

Bill

Misfortune
Misfortune

Rebecca slowly goes to the door and opens it.
Mill and Mr Hansen are on the other side.
Mill comes in first. She sees the situation and stops.
She is followed by Mr Hansen.
Mr Hansen is carrying a large wide-beamed torch, and wearing a protective coat.

Mr Hansen

For goodness sake.
What are you doing here?
You should have left long ago – everyone's gone already.
They're all on the ship, waiting for you.

Rebecca
Where's Francis?

Mr Hansen
On the ship.
I told you.
And the ship must leave. It's too dangerous.
You have to move.

Beat.

Mr Hansen
The island's been evacuated
You're the only two left.
The volcano could go off again at any moment.
If you don't come now I will have to tell the ship
to leave
NOW, Mr Lavarello.

Bill
The baby is dead

Mr Hansen stops.

Mr Hansen
I'm sorry

Pause.

Bill
And I is done it

Pause. Mr Hansen doesn't know what to say, he isn't even sure he understands.

Bill
I is killed it

Beat.

Bill
And now we is needing to . . .
We is needing to bury it

Bill turns around to face Rebecca, with some new energy.

Bill
We can't just be leaving it

Mr Hansen
Mr Lavarello you don't understand, you . . .

Bill
We is needing to bury her

Mr Hansen is too shocked and out of his depth to add anything.

Bill
I'll be taking it to the church
Is a vault
Was made when we built it

Mr Hansen
You can't get near the church
It's cut off
They've put up tape
It isn't safe

Bill starts to move with the baby.

Bill
I is going to try

Mr Hansen
Mr Lavarello you . . .

Mr Hansen physically stands in his path.

Mr Hansen
I can't let you
You'll be killed
Give me the baby, we can take it back to the boat

Bill
NO

Bill snatches it away.
They are in stalemate, neither person will let the other
near.
Mill steps out of the shadows and takes charge of the
situation.

Mill
I'll take it
I'll take them both
All three of them to the church
I is knowing a way is not taped off.

She holds out her arms for the baby.
Bill gives it to her.
She starts to walk out.
Bill and Rebecca follow her, suddenly like small children.

Mill (*to Mr Hansen*)
You is coming with us
And after . . .
We is coming back to the ship
Straight after
Together
And when we is getting back to the ship
You isn't saying a word
Not any of this to anyone
Is you clear?
Was born dead.
Is what we will say.
Is enough shouting and screaming
Is the whole world turning upside down already
Mr Hansen?
Was born dead.
Is things about the island that you isn't understanding
You isn't saying a word.

Mill, Bill and Rebecca leave.
Mr Hansen remains, stunned.

Mill, Bill, Rebecca and Mr Hansen in the vault under the church.
They have very little room and they are half in darkness.
The only light comes from Mr Hansen's wide-beamed torch, which he is holding so that Bill can see, but he himself is in shadow.
He is trying to be as removed as possible from the situation.
Bill is furiously digging, almost as if all the energy of the night before has found purpose.
Mill is watching him.
Rebecca is further away still.
Mr Hansen speaks, half under his breath and almost to himself.

Mr Hansen
We'll miss the boat

No one answers him.

Mr Hansen
They will leave without us if we don't . . .

Still no answer.
After a long pause Mill speaks.

Mill
Why?

The first time she says this it comes out as more of a croak. She tries again.

Mill
Why?
Bill?

Bill stops digging but won't look at her.

Mill

Be telling me there is a reason

Bill can't answer, so after a short pause he carries on digging.

Mr Hansen

If we miss the boat we . . .

Mr Hansen stops. Bill is still digging.
Eventually Bill manages to answer Mill but what he says he finds the hardest to say of all.

Bill

I is baptised it Mill
After
Was the worst
And the . . .
And the water
The water
Is the water that turned

He holds out his hands.

Bill

Is turned

Pause.

Mill

Was born dead, Bill.
Even to Francis
Was born dead.

Pause.
Then more quietly, almost to herself:

Mill

Don't stop digging
Keep on digging.
Keep on digging

End of Act One.

Act Two

SCENE ONE

Southampton, England. Eleven months have passed since Act One.
Inside Mr Hansen's jar factory.
Mill enters Mr Hansen's office in a flurry.

Mill
Is said I is needing an appointment.
Is said I is needing an appointment, and I is said I is
coming in.
Is said I is needing an appointment and hah, I is said
I isn't
Is said I is needing an appointment and I is said,
I isn't, I isn't when he is come smashing H'egg
in our kitchen, why is I needing one now?
And is looking at me, all eyes down his nose
But I is standing firm
And is said I is needing an appointment
Is said I is needing an appointment and . . .

Mr Hansen
Hallo Mill

Mill stops.

Mr Hansen
What can I do for you?

Mill
Be telling Francis I isn't needing an appointment

Mr Hansen
Sit down Mill

Mill
Mr Hansen is a friend of mine, I is told him. Is a

friend of mine, so don't be making appointments
when a friend is visiting a friend

Mr Hansen
I'll tell him

Mill
Mr Hansen is your boss he is saying
Is all hairs slick down his face.

Mr Hansen
I'll tell him, Mill.

Pause. Mill sits down.

Mr Hansen
What is wrong?

Pause.

Mill
Everybody is getting sick

Mr Hansen
Go on

Mill
Is said we'd be back by now and . . .
We is learnt to count the seasons here.
But some of the seasons is even having their second
count
And everyday the old people is saying to the young
people, 'Soon soon,
We'll be going back soon.'
And the young people is saying to the children,
'Soon soon.'
And the children is saying it to the old,
'Soon.'
And everyone is looking out of the window, always
looking out of the window, and the government
men is saying 'soon'
And people in shops, and even you is saying 'soon'

And I am here to be asking when?
When Mr Hansen?
You is said we is going back, but when?

Pause.

Mr Hansen

Maybe you should have made an appointment.

Mill

We is friends isn't we? You and me? You said we was
friends.

Pause.

Mill

Is it money? I know we is expensive and everyone is
always bringing us things, and everybody be
thinking those people from the island, is better if
they never come.

Mr Hansen

It's not money

Mill

So maybe you is worried about who will be doing
our jobs? Who'll be packing all the jars when we
is gone?

Mr Hansen

It's not the jobs Mill

Mill

Or the houses, maybe you is not sure who be living
in the houses . . .

Pause.
Mr Hansen looks at his watch.

Mr Hansen

I've got a meeting, any minute.
I am going to have to go.

Mill

I is only asking what everyone is asking.

Pause.

Mill

What I is told Francis to be asking.

Mr Hansen brings up a chair.

Mill

You is looking tired Mr Hansen

Mr Hansen

I am tired.

Mr Hansen points to a map on the wall.

Mr Hansen

See that Mill. You see all those crosses. Seven crosses, they are mine.
Seven factories.
Small factories, I'll admit but . . .
I am a business man, first and foremost.
You have to remember that.

Pause.

Mr Hansen

I am sorry that they are sick

Mill

Francis says is only because they is not trying that they is sick.
Francis says they is wanting to be sick.
Francis is saying we is wanting to be complaining, be saying hah H'England is a nonsense place, is wanting to be too frightened to be going out, but isn't true.
We isn't wanting that.
We is just wanting to go home

Beat.

Mill
Mr Hansen?
Is all we want.

Mr Hansen gets his breath.

Mr Hansen
But you can't, Mill.

Beat.

Mr Hansen
I'm sorry
You can't go home
It's not possible.

Mill
Why?

Mr Hansen
Because the island has gone.

Pause.

Mr Hansen
Maybe we should have told you before, but . . .
The volcano came right up over the village, and
buried it.

Pause.

Mr Hansen
The British Navy went out there. Quite soon after.
They sent a report to Mr Cavendish.

Mill
Nobody was telling us

Mr Hansen
We wanted you to settle in. To stop getting sick
That was the plan

Mill has to take this in.

Mill

Was Francis knowing already?

Mr Hansen

Yes.

Pause.

Mill

Is all gone?

Mr Hansen nods.

Even the meeting house? The school?

Mr Hansen

Yes

Mill

The church?

Mr Hansen

Yes

Mill

Is all gone?
Is all the houses, every single one?

Mr Hansen

Yes, Mill

Mill

Not even one left?

Mr Hansen

No

Mill

Not even my house?

Pause.

Mill

My house is gone, pff. My house is gone? Is buried,
is gone?

Mr Hansen

You have a house here.

Mill

My house is here?

Mill looks around.

Mill

So is my house here now? Is my house here, is this house with the rain is coming through the floors?

Mr Hansen

We can do something about the damp.

Mill

No more looking out of the window and thinking maybe is today?

Pause.

Mill

Maybe is soon soon. Is completely gone? You is sure?

Mill takes this in.

Mill

Is lucky we is left. Is lucky you is seen us from your ship with all the smoke, and was coming to get us, or else we is all gone.

Mill is upset, she starts to fiddle with her skirt.

Mill

But I is thinking is a shame. Is a shame about that volcano. Is such a shame

Pause.

Mill

Is such a shame about that volcano.

Mr Hansen

I am going to have to go, Mill.
I'm sorry.

Mill nods.

Mr Hansen
>You can stay in here if you want.
>Take as long as you want.

Mill
>Is such a shame.

Mr Hansen picks up his case.

Mr Hansen
>I know

Mill
>I is wishing we was still able to be looking out of the
>window and think soon soon.

Mr Hansen
>See, I should have waited a bit longer before telling you

Pause.

Mr Hansen
>I have to go
>It'll be alright Mill

Mill
>Is such a shame

He touches Mill's shoulder.
Beat.

Mr Hansen
>It'll be alright

He leaves.
Mill sits in silence.
*Then she starts speaking slowly, almost strangulated at
first.*

Mill
>Is no more looking out of the window
>And saying is soon

Is no crawfish and Pinnawin H'eggs
Is the Queen now,
And puddings
And is no more watching weeks and weeks for a boat,
and looking and
Looking
Is going up in a lift,
And wearing a mac
A mac-in-tosh
Is no more collecting sea shells
Is cinema on Sundays
And umbrellas
Is no more digging on the patches
Is train rides and baths
And is eating raspberries
And watching the trees
Is seeing them changing their colours and all the
leaves is orange
And is no more seaweed all over your shoes
Is flicking a switch and is light
And is music sometimes, is saying Hmm I is wanting
to listen to the music
And ding, is music
And is no more playing games with the children on
the shore
Is working
And is walking on the pavement and is seeing crowds
And is a football match, and is all jostling crowds,
and nobody is looking where they is walking and they
is treading on my feet and is squashing and is shouting
and always shouting
And is no more my father's old suit for weddings

Mill stops.
She starts again.

Mill
    And is puddings

Is the Queen on the television
Wearing a hat
And I is seen the trees, and all the leaves is going orange
And is no more seaweed, is flicking a switch and is light
And music
And is saying I is wanting to listen to music, ding is
music
And puddings and the Queen . . .
And football matches . . .
And puddings.

She wipes tears from her eyes.

Mill
And puddings

SCENE TWO

Francis and Bill in the factory boiler room.

Francis
You can pretend there are windows.
You understand how these dials work?
Uncle Bill is you listening?

Bill comes over.

Francis
You must listen to me.
You are wanting the job, aren't you?
Lots of people here don't have jobs, you're the lucky
one.
You just have to watch the pressure.
See here? If this drops below the red line, turn it.
Just a little. The marker should be staying between
those two lines.
If it goes the other way, turn the handle. Just a degree
or two.

It's all written down
Bill here, see is written on the side

Bill looks.

Bill
I's never had a job before
Only the patches.

Francis
Then the other thing is the temperature.
It's got to stay just at or around boiling.
Too cool and the machines stop working,
Too hot and the whole thing blows.
Ok?
Only it'll tell you if it goes wrong.
Is an alarm. Sounds like a bell.
You hear it, and you can adjust it again, by these
levers.
Too low and you pull this one,
Too high and the other.
Is easy.
All you have to do is make sure it all stays constant.
See?

Bill is looking around the pipes.

Bill
Is nothing like the patches

Francis
Forget about the patches.
It doesn't help.
Forget all about the patches.

Pause.

It's a good job Uncle Bill. I've got you a good job.

Bill
Is a lot of pipes

Francis

You sure you's understood everything?

Bill

Is a lot of water

Francis

Yes. Boiling water
Tonnes and tonnes of boiling water

Bill

Where does it come from?

Francis

I don't know.

Bill

Must come from somewhere. Before it is boiling
Are we near a river here?

Francis

Who knows?

There is a loud noise above them. Bill jumps and covers his head.

Francis

It does that sometimes.
Its only an air lock
It can make quite a din. You'll get used to it
You may need to take your jumper off, it can get
quite warm in here
I'll have to leave you now.
I've things to do.
It is a good job, Uncle Bill
You'll get used to it.
You're lucky to have it.

Francis leaves.
Bill is alone. The pipes make a noise, he looks around

SCENE THREE

Bill and Mill are sitting on deck chairs, in their garden.

Bill

This is what H'England people do Mill

Mill

I know

Bill

We is from H'England now

Mill

I know

Bill

Is you happy?

He looks at her.
She takes his hand.
They carry on sitting.
An aeroplane flies overhead.
Pause.

Mill

We needs to see it

She looks into the sky.

Mill

We can't just be saying, Ok is the end of it
We needs to be seeing it
Maybe we should be sending someone to see it
Then they come back and tell us
Is still our island isn't it?
Maybe there is some little part is Ok
Just a little part
We needs to see it

Pause.
Bill is still watching the sky, Mill looks up too.

Bill

Second aeroplane today

They both watch it for a second.

Bill

Sometimes seems like the smoke is dividing the sky

Pause.

Mill

Maybe we could be sending some back to see it
Some of us
Just a few
If we all was saving and put our money in
We could all be doing that, couldn't we?
Someone be collecting it
And someone else be buying the tickets
Then they could come back be telling us what is like
Then maybe we would all stop being sick
Bill?

Bill

Maybe

Mill

What do you think?

Bill

I don't know

Mill

Some of the women been saying I should be the one
Is organising it.

Bill gets up and goes over to the end of his garden.
He becomes obsessed by the possibility of water all
around, although there is no physical source on stage.

Bill

Where does that come from?

Mill

What?

Bill

There, this. All this . . .
Where does it come from?

*He picks up a patch of earth and squeezes it. The
moisture drips out.
He turns to face her.*

Bill

Are we near a river here?

Mill

I don't know

*He puts the patch of earth back.
Bill looks either way along the garden.*

Bill

I don't know either.

SCENE FOUR

*Rebecca is standing inside Mr Hansen's office.
It is after the end of the working day and nobody is there.
She looks around anxiously
She knocks on the table once or twice in case someone
is near.
No one appears, she looks around again.
Francis enters from a side door.
He is carrying a large bunch of keys and some files, etc.*

Francis

Mr Hansen has gone already.
You'll have to come back and see him another day.

Rebecca
I isn't wanting to see Mr Hansen.

Pause.

Francis
Well no one else here, everyone's gone

Rebecca doesn't move

Francis
I'll be locking up in a minute
Whatever you want will have to keep until tomorrow

Rebecca still shows no intention of moving.

Francis
Didn't you hear me?
You will have to go home.

Pause.

Rebecca
I is learning to read

Beat.

Rebecca
Yes, I is reading now

Francis
I'm busy, can't you see?

Rebecca
Can spell all sorts of things now

Francis
Good, excuse me

Rebecca
Can spell 'Francis'.

Francis
Excuse me, I have to do this

Rebecca
Sometimes I can spell 'Francis', sometimes 'Francis' isn't wanting to be spelt.

Francis
Go home Rebecca

Rebecca
I is only wanting to be talking to you
Nothing else, just is talking

Francis
There is nothing to talk about
Is there?
I don't remember there being anything to talk about

Pause.

Rebecca
Everybody been saying how different you is now.
Everyone been saying you is the man we won't recognize, is saying he looks like Francis but isn't Francis, if you were speaking to him you would never be knowing, is this person is working hard always always working hard, doing so well

Pause

Rebecca
I is just wanting to be talking Francis
I is remembering when you were telling me about the piece of glass you kept in your pocket.
You still keeping that piece of glass in your pocket?

Beat.

That you was turning when you needed to be remembering how to change.

Francis
I don't remember.

Rebecca
Before

Francis
I don't remember

Rebecca
Is last time you left.

Francis
I don't remember.
I don't remember anything from before.
Nothing
Even you.
And it is 'I am' not 'I is', if you want to be talking at least be talking properly.

Pause.

Rebecca
You do remember me

Francis
You need to go now.
We both need to go. I have a lot to get on with

Rebecca
We were marked out from birth Francis

Francis
Look, you shouldn't be here.
The office is closed.
You can be coming back to see Mr Hansen another time.
Please don't try to be talking to me.

Rebecca
I miss you.
Is all.

Francis stops.
He looks at her.

Rebecca
Francis?

Pause.

Rebecca
I is alone as you is here

Pause.

Francis
No.
If you're alone that's because that was what you
wanted.

Beat

Francis
You wanted this.
Not me
All those months I wanted to talk
You wouldn't come near.
You wanted this

Rebecca
Please, Francis,
I wasn't knowing what I wanted.

Francis
Its too late
Anyway I'm not alone. Why should I be alone?
Don't think I am alone Rebecca
I am not alone
Out there is all of H'England.

SCENE FIVE

*Bill is in the boiler room by himself, walking round the
room and looking at the pipes.
There is the din of the air lock. Bill jumps.*

SCENE SIX

Mill and Mr Hansen meet in a café. Mill is carrying the briefcase that Mr Hansen gave her in Act One.

Mr Hansen
Come in, I won't bite

Mill doesn't sit.

Mill
I thought you was very busy

Mr Hansen
Let me buy you a coffee

Mill
No

Mr Hansen
Sounds like you have been busy too

Mill shrugs.

Mr Hansen
How is it going?

Mill
Is just an idea

Mr Hansen
It's a good one

Pause.

Mr Hansen
It'll be hard work. A lot of money

Mill
Never been minding hard work. Is got to see it
Mr Hansen.

Mr Hansen
Of course.

Its just,
It's very enterprising that is all. How much have you
got to raise then?

Mill

Hundreds.

Mr Hansen

How many will be going?

Mill

Six

Mr Hansen

Splendid

Mill

And a camera

Mr Hansen

Good for you Mill.
Come on Mill, let me buy you a coffee.
Or a tea, maybe you'd prefer a tea?
I've got some news for you

Mill

Oh?

Mr Hansen

That is better
I want you to stop frowning.
You've got such a wonderful face if you stop frowning
I passed the message on about the houses
And the damp, it all went through

Mill

Oh.

Mr Hansen

They said it is in hand
They said they will consider it
They will consider it Mill, they want you to be happy

Mill sits down.

Mill
Hot chocolate.

Mr Hansen
When you stop frowning your whole face lights up,
do you know that?

Mill
And a pudding

Mr Hansen laughs. He relaxes a little.

Mr Hansen
Prime sites
All over the city, if it goes through. New houses Mill,
that is what we are talking
New houses Mill.
Built for you

Mill
Why?

Mr Hansen
Isn't that what you wanted?
You said the houses were no good
Rain was coming through the floor

Mill
Why?

Mr Hansen
What do you mean why?

Mill
Why now?
We is been living in them already for is nearly a year

Mr Hansen
These things take time, they've come through now
that is the main thing.

Mill

What about the money for them?
They isn't coming free is they?

Mr Hansen

That will all be sorted, remember this is only a
proposal at this stage.
We'll sort that out later.
Let me explain. The front door, inside a hall. Maybe
a fitted carpet, maybe a lino floor, cork, who knows.
Further down, a living room. Open fire or maybe
central heating. To the end a fitted kitchen, and off
that a dining room – for dinner parties, whatever.
Upstairs bedroom one, the master, bedroom two,
for the children, and bedroom three a spare. Outside
garden to the back, along the side a double garage,
even a patio.

Mill

Where is all this money going to be coming from?

Mr Hansen

Have you ever seen a fitted kitchen Mill?

Pause.

Mr Hansen

So we want this to go through yes?
We want them to make the deal, there's some things
we can do to help
Mill don't look like that, you've got your worried
face on again.
Stop frowning
It's not going to be a problem
Ok? Keep smiling, its not going to be a problem
If the deal goes through it going to be a straight gift,
well nearly a gift they'll be some rent. Of course
there will need to be some rent
But it would be very knocked-down prices

Mill

We is not going to stop getting the six passages

Mr Hansen

Nobody is asking you to

Of course they are not

Nobody

You need to see the island one last time, or a picture
of the island, everyone can understand that, it's a
shame the navy didn't take photographs when they
went and then it would have saved you all this
trouble, but even still everyone can understand it.
I can understand it, but . . .

Postpone it

Take the houses. Settle in

Wait six months

Then send the men, and women

You'll get your pictures

It is to do with attitude, Mr Cavendish and his team

They want to know you are Britons

That you see yourself as Britons

You know what I am talking about

Start dressing a little like Britons

Even when you are by yourselves feel like Britons

At night

Even when you are undressed, that is the thing.

When you are naked.

Be Britons even under all the layers

Its good to be Briton Mill

And the passages back to the island

It's part of the same thing

Just let the dust settle

Postpone it

It's just not good timing

Six men out of the community

It's not good timing

Mill gets up.

Mr Hansen
Will you think about it?
I'm working hard for you all Mill.

Mill
Is you ever doing magic any more Mr Hansen?

Mr Hansen
No

Mill
Is a pity
I was preferring you much more when you did magic

Mill starts to walk out.

Mr Hansen
What do you mean?
Don't just leave, Mill?
What do you mean?
Mill?

Mr Hansen in his frustration grabs Mill's arm a little too roughly.
He realises what he has done.
He lets her go.

Mr Hansen
Mill?

Mill leaves.

SCENE SEVEN

Mill sitting on one of the H'England chairs outside. She is working, counting money.
Rebecca is sitting on another of the chairs.

Mill
You is always in trouble girl.

Rebecca

    Is never anyone wanting to talk to me
    That was why

Mill

    Be keeping an eye out for Francis.
    Can you see Francis?

Rebecca

    No.
    Wasn't wanting to be alone.
    I didn't know who they was.

Pause.

Rebecca

    Was a woman there
    That was only why
    They was the only people be talking to me
    She had a nice face
    I didn't know they had a camera
    Hair all shiny
    She was wanting to talk to me
    Didn't know she was from a paper
    Say let's be seeing you smiling island girl.
    Let's be seeing you smile.

Pause.

Rebecca

    But then they is mean
    The woman was mean.
    They is laughing at me next.
    And they is asking all these questions, trying to
    confuse me
    All these questions

Mill

    You shouldn't have hit her.

Rebecca
And I was telling her I didn't know the answers.
Is things I didn't know what she was talking about.

Mill
You shouldn't be talking to those people Rebecca

Rebecca
Then she said I must be simple was why I didn't know
Said all the islanders were simple.

Mill
Is said that?

Rebecca
Yes.
Said because we is all inbred too much.
Is never hit anyone before

Mill
Is said we is inbred?

Rebecca
Yes

Mill
How hard is you hit her?

Rebecca shrugs.

Mill
How hard?

Rebecca
Is very hard.

Mill laughs.

Rebecca
Is made my hand go all red.

Mill laughs louder.
So does Rebecca.
Mill sees Francis. She calls him over.

Mill
Francis!

Rebecca
Don't be calling him.
Don't want him to be knowing.

Mill
Needing a word is all.

Francis enters.

Francis
Yes. What is it?

Mill
Don't say it like that Francis
Isn't an appointment system here.
Is needing a word is all

Francis sits down.

Mill
Be pouring Francis some H'England tea out of the
H'England pot Rebecca.
Gently.

Francis
I haven't got long.

Mill
Spend a minute Francis.

Rebecca pours some H'England tea.

Mill
And using the H'England saucers Rebecca.
Rebecca?

Rebecca reluctantly does so.

Mill
I is had an idea

Francis

Oh?

Mill

Rebecca and giving Francis some H'England milk out
of the H'England jug.

*Rebecca pours the milk. Francis and Rebecca are
awkward with each other.*

Mill

I is nearly raised the money now

Francis

You know what I think

Mill

Listen to me Francis

Francis

Hasn't Mr Hansen talked to you?

Mill

Rebecca be giving Francis a H'England biscuit out
of the H'England jar

Francis

No

Mill

Eat a biscuit Francis
Francis?

Rebecca passes Francis a biscuit.
Francis starts to eat it.

Mill

I is nearly raised the money now
Is nearly got enough for the six to be going back.
Just to be looking.
And I is wanting to ask you would you be one of
them?

Pause.

Mill

Think about it first
I know is a big thing to ask.
But I is too old, and Bill . . .

Francis

You know the answer.

Mill

Is as easy as that, is not thinking about it?

Pause.

Mill

I would like it to be being you.
I trusts you Francis

Beat.

Mill

Rebecca be giving Francis some more H'England tea,
And a bit of H'England sugar.

Francis

No Mill
NO
You know what I think
You aren't being sensible about this
What about the houses?
You need the houses badly.
Look at them. You should take the offer.
How else are you going to be affording them?

Mill

We need to be seeing it Francis

Francis

Why?
Can't you imagine what a buried island looks like?
Can't you surely?

A lump of rock.
So what?
It's a lump of rock now.
And who needs to see that?

Mill shakes her head.

Mill

I is sorry I asked you Francis
I is sorry I is wasted your time
Rebecca Francis is finished his tea now.

Francis

I'm not saying you wasted my time.

Mill

Go on you don't want to go
Rebecca he is finished his biscuit.

Francis

It just makes no sense

Mill

Not to you

Francis

We just need to leave it behind now

Mill

Rebecca he is finished with his H'England cup now
Good-bye Francis, go and do what you have to do

Francis

They'll stop you anyway.
You know that?
You can't just walk in and buy six passages.
What, back to the island and you don't think they
will realise?
They'll stop them
They said they don't want you to go back at the
moment and they mean it
They will say the boat is full up or something,

I promise you
They are like that, you don't understand
They won't get back
It's the truth Mill, I'm only telling you the truth

Mill
Off you go

Francis
Don't be shutting me out Mill

Mill
You is shutting yourself out Francis

Francis
No
Is you that shut me out

Pause.

Francis
You are right I have finished my tea

He gives the tea cup back.
He leaves.
Mill and Rebecca look the way he went.

Rebecca
Has all of H'England now, is what he told me.

Pause.

Mill
We need someone who can be helping us.
If Francis won't then someone else.

Another aeroplane goes overhead.
They both look up.

Mill
Who is these people again?

Rebecca
Which people?

Mill

Your people. The people is from the paper
With the camera.
The one that you hit.

Rebecca

No
They is mean
They think we is simple

Mill

They won't be thinking that when they sees all the
money we is raised
What is the name of the people?

Rebecca

You can't go to them

Mill

We is having to get these passages Rebecca
And if Francis won't help . . .

Rebecca

No

Mill

Maybe one of them could even be coming with us
Could be using their camera.

Rebecca

Is only one thing about us they are interested in.
I isn't thinking you will be wanting to be telling it
Not for no number of passages

Mill

What?

Rebecca

Is why I hate them
Is why I hit her.

Mill
Rebecca?

Rebecca
I is said I isn't knowing
Is only the old ones knowing

Mill
About what?

Rebecca
I shouldn't have been talking to her

Mill
Tell me
Rebecca?

Rebecca
Something on the island

Mill
What is on the island?

Rebecca
Something is happened on the island a long time ago
Something bad
Something bad even before I is bad
Is all I know
Something before the baptisms

Pause.

Rebecca
You know what I is meaning now?
Before Mr Lavarello is gone and come back with the church.

Beat.

Mill
And they was asking you about it?

Rebecca
  Yes

Mill
  So what was you saying?

Rebecca
  I is said I didn't know

Mill
  And what was they saying?

Rebecca
  They is said find out

Mill
  And what was you saying?

Rebecca
  I is said what if it is something bad

Mill
  And what is they saying?

Rebecca
  Is said it doesn't matter
  They is said I wasn't even to be seeing them again
  until I was knowing
  They said maybe I was too simple to be finding out

Mill thinks about this.

Mill
  We need to get those passages

Pause.

Rebecca
  No, Mill.

Mill
  We is needing those passages Rebecca.
  We is never going to be able to live here until we is
  seen the island

Seen it buried
Seen just how buried
Seen it for certain sure.

Pause.

Mill

I'll have to be asking Bill.

SCENE EIGHT

Bill alone in the boiler room.
Mr Hansen enters.

Mr Hansen

Sorry, you're busy
I . . .
I'm not disturbing anything am I?
I don't mean to disturb you
I'm a good boss Bill
Don't think I don't care
I do care

Bill doesn't say anything so Mr Hansen comes in.

Mr Hansen

It's funny, I own this whole place and it took me a
while to find you

*Mr Hansen is rambling, he wanders around not sure
what to do.*

Mr Hansen

I heard you were the self-appointed chaplain on the
island
I didn't know that
Maybe you, maybe you understand
What it is like to be the boss
All this and . . .
Do you think I have changed Bill?

I look at myself and I don't feel changed
But I . . .

He smiles, he's embarrassed.

Mr Hansen
Christ you were the chaplain . . .
The chaplain
I was surprised when I heard that
You?
Well I don't need to
But I haven't forgotten,
Its right up here in my . . .
Maybe that was when I changed
I should have said something
At the time, done something
After what I . . .
What you told me.
Why didn't I do anything?
What kind of man am I? I didn't say anything.
Didn't tell anyone.
Didn't say a bloody word.
What kind of man does that make me?
You answer me that?
What kind of man?

Pause.

Mr Hansen
I am a good employer Bill, I care about people
I'm a fair man Bill

Pause.

Mr Hansen
When you were chaplain
Did you have people come to see you, to tell you
things?
I have a confession
A real one

Something I . . .
Well I need to get it off my chest
And I know you would understand
That is what they say isn't it? 'I need to get this off
my chest, father'?
In the movies
Sorry, not father, I know
Just chaplain
Chap-lain
Like I said I have a confession
And if I tell you, maybe then . . .

Beat.

Mr Hansen
I lied
Bill did you hear me?
I lied
I lied to Mill
Of all people to Mill
Straight to her face
Not only that but . . .
I told you I needed to get it off my chest
I was paid to do it
Not paid exactly, not cash up front but
I got prettily heavily rewarded for it

Beat.

Mr Hansen
I told Mill that the island was destroyed
And I told Francis
And through them I told all of you
The island is . . .
Well it's not.
The lava only came to the foot of the mountain
Everything else is fine
The navy did go there and that is what they found
I've known for ages

Since you arrived practically
There are other reasons why they don't want you to
go back
Oh and the best thing, the church
The lava came right up to the door of the church and
stopped
Right there by the door
Even I would say that that was a miracle
Anyway there is no physical reason why you shouldn't
all go back
Tomorrow
No earthly reason
Except, well . . .
The island is a pretty handy piece of land for
Did you see the war?
You heard of Hiroshima?
Nagasaki?
Well they . . .
They are developing them all the time
And a piece of land like that
No people
Miles from anywhere
Surrounded by sea
Secret
So Mr Cavendish
Well not just Mr Cavendish, but he is the man I deal
with
Drew up a plan
Which involved jobs, houses
My bank balance
Defence is big money
A fake report
All the information that has circulated about
volcanoes
Untrue, or at least untrue in your case
Your volcano turned out to be a sleepy little number

Fierce bark, but no bite
And now . . .
Hardly a smolder
All I had to do was tell you all.
But you mustn't know this
You don't know any of this
You are in role as my confessor
What's the word?
Confidante
As I was yours
You can be silent
You can take this with you to the grave
We can both have sleepless nights
We can both see the people around us unhappy
You say a word, and I'll tell
Francis or the police or . . .
Who knows who.
The world if necessary.
About you.
The night before we left the island.
In the church

Pause.

Mr Hansen
Is that fair?
Don't think I don't care about you Bill
I do care about you, I care about all of you
Maybe even too much

Bill
Did you hold a gun?

Mr Hansen
What?

Bill
In the war?
You is said you is seen the war.

146

Beat.

Bill
    Did you hold a gun?

Beat.

Mr Hansen
    Yes
    Did you?

SCENE NINE

Bill and Mill come outside.
Mill is leading Bill into the sunlight, he looks somewhat dazed.

Mill
    Don't always be looking at the canal Bill,
    Is a much better view this way
    Come on, I'll set up the H'England chairs.

She sees the chairs are destroyed.

Mill
    Oh

She tries to pick them up.

Mill
    Is the wind
    Must be the wind last night
    The wind and the rain

Bill
    Hold my hand

Mill holds Bill's hand.
Tears come into his eyes.

Mill
    Is only the H'England chairs Bill

We can get some more
Don't cry
We'll get some more Bill, I'll get them

Bill stops crying, almost as if his sadness overwhelms the tears.

Mill

I'll get some chairs from the kitchen
We can still sit outside can't we? Like the H'England people do?

Mill goes inside.
Bill stands there helpless.
Mill comes back with kitchen chairs.

Mill

Must have been the wind

She puts the chairs side by side.
They sit.
Bill takes her hand again.
Mill squeezes Bill's hand, then puts her hands back on her lap.

Mill

Is something important I need to tell you
Ask you.

Pause.

Mill

I need to break a promise
I need to tell them about the time, before the baptisms

Pause.

Bill

Tell who?

Mill

The papers here
Is years ago I know,

Years and years
They is half knowing already, someone is told them
something
I need the help of the papers to get the passages
We won't get the passages else,
Not them and the houses
And they will keep stopping them
They'll say the boat was full up
So Francis says
If we go to the papers, then they'll have to let us go
And we need to see the island

Bill can't speak.

Mill

Only they want to know something
Is what they want
Is like a swap

Pause.

Mill

I won't tell them everything
I won't tell them about you
Not if you don't want me to
It was all of us, anyway

Bill holds his head in his hands.

Bill

Can you hear pipes Mill?
I think I can hear pipes
Not just at work, all the time now
I is going to buy a map, Mill
See if we are near a river
Or maybe the sea . . .

Mill

Talk to me Bill

Pause.

Bill
All the time
Not just at work now

Mill
Talk to me?

Mill realises there is no possibility.

Mill
Just the basics, that's all I'll tell them

Bill
Was the worst, was the very worst

Mill
I know but then after you went away and is come
back came the baptisms
You can't blame yourself Bill
It wasn't just you
Was all of us
We needed you to be the strong one
We might have all of died
You were, you were the strong one
Is no one ever blaming you
You did what you had to do
You did what was the right thing

Bill
All my life I is done the wrong thing

Mill
It was the right thing Bill
It was the right right thing
It was the right thing

Bill
And what about the baby?
Was that the right thing too?

Bill alone in the boiler room.
He looks about him. He touches the dials.

Bill

    Is there a river near here?
    Is there a river near here?

The pipes scream at him. He screams back.

Bill

    IS THERE A RIVER?

SCENE ELEVEN

Mill enters Mr Hansen's office.
Mr Hansen is looking out of the window. Silence.
She sits down.
Mr Hansen brings his attention to her.

Mill

    I want you to write something down for me

Mr Hansen

    I watched you out of the window Mill,
    I could see you walking practically all the way from
    your house to here
    Your walk has changed, do you know that?

Mill

    Will you take pen and paper, I need you to write
    something down for me.

Mr Hansen

    You stride now

Mill looks down at herself.
Then she looks back at Mr Hansen.

Mill

Take pen and paper

Mr Hansen

You even look different.
Your face
Did you have those lines before?
On your brow?
They aren't frown lines, they are new lines.

Mill goes to his desk, she picks up a piece of paper and a pen.
She gives them to him.

Mill

Write

Mr Hansen

What shall I say?

Mill

I'll tell you
I've got their names here
Is the ones Rebecca hit

She gets out a folded scrap of newspaper.

Mr Hansen

I don't know why you are doing this
You don't have to have any more to do with them

Mill

Is the only way we are going to get the passages
You be writing, I'll be talking
Read their names for me

Mr Hansen takes the scrap of paper.

Mr Hansen

Cooper and Blanchard
Celia Blanchard. I've heard of her.
She's no good Mill

Mill

She is going to help us
Write
Dear . . . Miss Celia Blanchard and Mr Cooper
Sorry about your punch, start with that.
Then put, was a time before the baptisms
Have you got that?

Mr Hansen

Yes

Mill

Was the time that no boat came
And no boat came, and no boat came
And even after years and years, no boat was coming
Is all very well for people in H'England to be thinking
we did a bad thing,
But there was no boat coming
No boat coming Mr Hansen.
They doesn't know what it is like when there is no
boat coming
Is you getting all this?

Mr Hansen nods.

Mill

And every day everyone has to be thinking this is
the day
And still no boat is coming
At first was Ok because we had plenty of crawfish
But then the crawfish season was over
But we still had the potatoes
Then the potatoes was over
So we ate the pinnawins
Then the pinnawins were over
And still no boat was coming
You is still writing?

Mr Hansen

    Don't tell them this Mill.
    Whatever happened, it's your business

Mill

    I want to tell them
    What we is done we is done
    I is not ashamed of what we is done.
    I know all of H'England doesn't think much of our
    little island
    But I isn't ashamed of what we is done
    The pinnawins were over, you is got that?
    Then was the stormy season coming and we knew
    that if we didn't have no boat before, there would
    be no boat till after the storms had gone.
    Certainly there would be no boat until for four months
    Not even a chance
    And we knew that we had to get through four months
    And we looked at the food we is had left
    And we is counted
    And we is counted all the heads
    And we is divided, so each person has a little bit of
    food for all the months
    But is no way
    Is no way that the food we is got left is going to do
    for all the heads for all the months until the end of
    the stormy season
    And even then we isn't certain that we is going to get
    a boat
    So we is all going to die
    That is what we is thinking
    Is you still writing?

Mr Hansen

    Yes

Mill

    Then someone had an idea

154

No point in everyone dying
I is never sure who said it first
But others is agreeing
Some of us can live
Is enough food for some of us to live
And so we is counted again
And we is worked out that the bigger proportion can
live
If the smaller proportion . . .
Seventeen people
People don't understand here what it is like when
there is no boat come
Don't understand what it is like to have no food
So was decided everyone put a button in a box and
draw out the buttons,
The first lot of buttons drawn out, they is the people
that live
The second lot, those seventeen . . .
They don't.
So was what we is done,
And then there is all this trouble about the buttons
everyone has to make sure that they have a button
is like no one else's
Eventually we all has a button,
And we all put a button in the box
And each button be drawn out
One person is drawing them all out
And we is told if your button is drawn out is the end
of it
Is no swapping
And we is all singing
Is a strange sort of singing we is done that day
I don't think is called singing really
And he is drawing the first few buttons
Then is drawn more and more
Mine is drawn, and Bill's is drawn

And everyone that is drawn out first is jumping for joy
Is weeping, just because they is Ok
But those who isn't drawn
They just keeps on sitting there
Their faces is like stone
And they is not laughing
And eventually all the buttons that is going to be
drawn is drawn
And those that is not drawn, is not drawn
My sister is there
Her eyes is so wide
But she is not crying
And that same day their food is re-divided
But the rest of us
We couldn't just watch them die
We couldn't just carry on with the rest of us living
At first we thought maybe put them somewhere
In one house
Then someone else had an idea
Is the right idea, even though he is never forgiven
himself
And he is got out the boat and he is told them to get
in the boat
And all those people is got in the boat,
All seventeen
Some of them is so weak already he is had to carry
them to the boat
And they is all sat there – rows and rows
Empty faces, old old faces
Is got so old all of a sudden
Even though my sister is younger than me, her face is
all bone
And we is said good bye on the shore
And then he is rowed them round to the other side of
the island
Is cut off – can only get there by sea

Is a path, but is ugly
And he is rowed them there and is left them, with the
little boat
And he is come back.
Is taken the ugly road through the mountain,
Is walked by the lake
And is come back without them

Pause.

Mill
And we is waited
And is the end of the stormy season
And there is a boat
Is a boat
And the boat is bring us food. Food and food
And we is asking why is we been forgotten?
Why is a boat not come for so long?
Why is no one brought us food?
And they told us there is a terrible war going on
All the world was at war
All the different countries is fighting
That is why they forgot to send a boat
They is been so busy
And Bill is gone back with them to see this war
And he came back with the church
And the baptisms
But the people is left on the other side of the island . . .
Was long long dead
We was doing the right thing

Mr Hansen has stopped writing, he is listening instead.

Mr Hansen
Don't tell them this Mill

Mill
We need the passages

Mr Hansen
I'll get you the passages
Don't tell them this

Mill wipes the tears from her eyes.

Mill
When you live on the island you know what is like
when no boat comes

Pause.

Mill
You write that down, we isn't ashamed of what we
is done
We isn't ashamed.

Mill wipes her tears.
Mr Hansen sees her do this and gives her his
handkerchief.

Mr Hansen
Don't tell this to the papers Mill

There is a loud noise outside the door.
Francis comes in, he is in a panic.

Francis
You'd better come

Mr Hansen
Why?

Francis
There has been an accident

Mr Hansen
Where?

Francis
Downstairs
In the boiler room

Mr Hansen
   What?

Francis
   Someone has locked themselves in
   I think you had better both come
   I think it might be Bill

SCENE TWELVE

Bill, locked in the boiler room.
He turns all the dials at once.
The alarm sounds.
Boiling water spurts out from many different pipes at
once and all over him.
It starts to fill the room, drowning him.

SCENE THIRTEEN

A few days later.
Mill is getting dressed.
She is in her island clothes again and holding the suit
that we saw Francis wear in Act One.
She is looking in the mirror.

Mill
   Is no more puddings
   Is no more anything sweet

Francis comes in. He is carrying a flower.
He tries to give it to Mill but she doesn't take it.
He puts it down.
Francis is still in H'England clothes.

Francis
   Mr Hansen is outside

Mill takes the jacket.

Mill

Bill was wearing this the day he is married me. You
know that?
Is my father's before him
All the men is worn it, but Bill . . .
Bill is looking the best by far

Francis

He says he will wait all day

Mill

You be wearing it Francis, just today

She tries to put it on him.

Francis

He let us all down Mill
Me as well

Mill takes it back.
Mill start to put it on herself.

Mill

Was fitting him the best
Better even really than it was fitting my father and
it was his suit

She starts to put on the trousers as well, over her clothes.

Mill

I is not gone mad Francis

She looks in the mirror.
She laughs.
She takes off the trousers.

Mill

Bill should be wearing it now
Tell them Bill should be wearing this
And when I is died I should be wearing the dress
I was wearing when we was wed

And even though we'll be in patches of earth on
the other sides of the world, maybe it won't seem
so far
Not so very very far
He was going to make old bones
Him and me and the patches.
Old bones.

She takes the jacket off.

Mill

Stupid stupid man

She nearly breaks down.
She stops herself.
She looks at Francis.

Mill

I is nothing to say to Mr Hansen
Today is the day I is burying my Bill

Pause.

Mill

Maybe I should be putting this suit on top of his
coffin?
Cover him like is a blanket

Mill picks up the flower and starts to put it in her lapel.

Mill

Go and tell Mr Hansen I is nothing to say to him

Francis

What did you tell him?

Mill looks at him.

Francis

Mill?

Mill

Is nothing

Francis

Must be something is made him change

Mill

Is something is gone now

Francis

Is about my mother?

Mill

Don't, Francis

Francis

Is about how my mother died

Mill carries on arranging her flower, but she is getting upset.

Francis

Is something about how all those people died.
And the baptisms, I know it has something to do
with the baptisms

Mill

NO.

Francis

Why can you tell Mr Hansen but you can't tell me?

Mill

Francis.

She holds his head tight. She kisses him.

Mill

Today is the day I am burying my Bill.
Please?
Today is the day we are burying our Bill.
Francis.
Not today.

Francis

Anyway

You don't need to tell me,
I know already.
I've always known.

*Francis kisses her, he is not being cruel, merely
acknowledging the gulf between them now.
He starts to walks out.*

Mill
He is loved you though

Quieter.

Mill
Always.
He is always loved all of us.

*Francis has gone.
Mill is left in front of the mirror.
She puts the jacket on.
She looks in the mirror again.
She cries.
Someone knocks.
She takes the jacket off.
Mr Hansen walks in.
Mill sees him and looks back to the mirror.
She picks up the flower and starts arranging it in her
lapel.*

Mill
I was telling Francis to tell you I would be speaking
to you some other day

Mr Hansen
I never meant to lie to you Mill
I know I did
Of course I know I did
But I never meant to

Mill starts to brush her hair.

Mill
I is on my way to the church

Mr Hansen
I know

Mill
Today is the funeral of my Bill

Mr Hansen
I know

Pause.

Mr Hansen
So it's a certainty you'll go back then?

Mill
We is having a vote

Mr Hansen
It's a certainty

Mill
Some are saying they want to stay

Mr Hansen
But you will be going whatever?

Pause.

Mr Hansen
I'll probably never see you again. You know that?
Probably never see any of you
Those that go
Those that stay I expect I will be saddled with for a
long time yet

Mill
I don't want some to be staying and some to be going

Pause.

Mill

If we is gone back straight away we would have all
gone.

Mr Hansen

I'm sorry Mill
I am sorry
You could stay
There is still the offer of houses if you want to . . .
I know
Of course you don't

Pause.
Mr Hansen gets out an egg.

Mr Hansen

I've got something to show you
Have you got my hankie still?

Mill

I don't want to be seeing it

Mr Hansen

I can do it again
The magic has come back
All I need is my hankie

Mill

Is not magic, anyway.
Is a trick

Mr Hansen puts the egg away.

Mr Hansen

It wasn't my fault
Anyone would have done the same
What is it about that bloody place?
You, all of you
What the hell is it about all of you?
I let you under my skin
That is what it is

Like thousands of tiny pinpricks
So I did some business, so what?

Beat.

Mr Hansen

When I walked on that black sand something happened
to me.
That bloody black sand
What is it about it?
I've kept some you know, as a momento
I collected it while I was there

Mill

You shouldn't have been taken it

Mr Hansen

I wanted it
Mill
I wanted it
I wanted what you have
I wanted the whole thing
I even wanted you

Pause.

Mr Hansen

I don't have an excuse
I know I let you down
That was all I came to say really

Mill

Today is the day I am burying my Bill

Mr Hansen

I'll probably never see you again

Mill picks up the suit jacket, she shows him.

Mill

He wore it the day we was getting married

Mr Hansen
    Will I?
    I'll probably never see you again

Mr Hansen starts to leave.

Mr Hansen
    Good-bye Mill

As Mr Hansen leaves, Mill shouts.

Mill
    He was a good man Mr Hansen

Mr Hansen stops and turns.

Mr Hansen
    There won't ever be a year without a boat Mill
    Even if only one of you goes back
    I'll make sure the ships keep coming
    As long as I'm alive, I can promise you that

SCENE FOURTEEN

By the docks.
Francis is standing by himself.
Rebecca comes up to him. She is wrapped up for the cold, and carrying bags.

Francis
    Is everyone going?

Rebecca
    Yes.

Francis
    I thought they . . .

Rebecca
    They's changed their minds
    They looked at this place and opened their eyes

Beat.

Francis
And you?

Rebecca
Me?
I is going because I is like nothing here.
Like a person is never existed.

Rebecca picks up her bags and moves on.

Francis
I didn't vote
I couldn't
I went in, I had the piece of paper in front of me
I saw the question.
'Do you want to return to the island?' and a big
YES and a big NO
And I couldn't do it
I couldn't decide.

Rebecca
I has to get to the boat

Pause.

Francis
Tell me what to do.
Rebecca?
Tell me what to do?

Rebecca gives him her attention properly for the first time.

Rebecca
You've never asked me anything, so don't go starting
now

Francis
Would you stay here with me?

Beat.

Francis
    I could get another job.
    Up North.
    We could go together.

Rebecca
    Is too long ago Francis
    As you said, is too late
    You and me
    Was another lifetime ago.

Beat.

Francis
    Or I could come with you
    If you want
    I could come back with you

Rebecca
    No

Francis
    Please Rebecca, tell me

Rebecca
    No Francis

Francis
    I want to hold you

Rebecca
    Francis?

Francis
    I is made a mistake
    All of it is a mistake.
    I was angry with you that was all.
    I don't want you to go.

Rebecca
    You'll be thinking about me until I'm over the horizon,
    then you'll forget

Francis
No

Rebecca
I've got to go Francis

Francis
I'll be coming with you, you just say the word

Rebecca
No Francis
You isn't wanting that
And I isn't wanting you if you isn't wanting that
It isn't me that you want
Not really
I know what it will be like, you'll be coming back for
a bit maybe, is staying for while, and maybe things
is nice but then in a few years a ship will be coming
and you'll be going off again.
We is missed our time, you and I.

Francis
That's not true

Rebecca
Is true Francis
You could spend your life running between one and
the other and not really living in either

Pause.

Choose
But be choosing for good
Look around you, is this what you is wanting?
Is it?
I is got to go

She starts to leave.

Francis
Rebecca?

Rebecca
    I'll be waving

She comes back and kisses him, gently.

Rebecca
    I'll be waving.
    I'll be waving Francis.